Plant a Natural
WOODLAND

'Every scrap of biological diversity is priceless,
to be learned and cherished,
and never to be surrendered without a struggle.'

Edward O. Wilson

Alone in the woods I felt
The bitter hostilities of the sky and trees
Nature has taught her creatures to hate…
…nature is sick at man
Sick at his fuss and fume
Sick at his agonies
Sick at his gaudy mind
That drives his body
Ever more quickly
More and more
In the wrong direction.

**From *Alone in the Woods*
by Stevie Smith**

Above: Rosa canina. *There are many species of native wild rose. They are more often found in hedgerows but will also grow along woodland verges, and even up trees. Illustrations also appear on page 7 (Rosa avensis) and page 128 (Rosa tomentosa), and the picture on page 123 is of rose hips in winter. Wild roses produce excellent food for birds.*

Plant a Natural
WOODLAND

A Handbook of Native Trees and Shrubs

CHARLOTTE DE LA BÉDOYÈRE

SEARCH PRESS

First published in Great Britain 2001

Search Press Limited
Wellwood, North Farm Road,
Tunbridge Wells, Kent TN2 3DR

Text copyright © Charlotte de la Bédoyère 2001; photographs
© Charlotte de la Bédoyère unless otherwise indicated

ISBN 0855 329 831

Page 1

*An ancient pollarded Beech (*Fagus sylvatica)

Pages 4–5

*Semi-mature Silver Birch (*Betula pendula)

Page 6

Bark of the Populus nigra

Page 7

*Left: Woodland scene with mature Small-leaved Lime (*Tilia cordata);
Right: Rosa avensis

Page 8

In the Woods *by Asher B. Durand (1796–1886)*

*The Metropolitan Museum of Art, New York, gift in memory of
Jonathan Sturges, by his children, 1895.*

Pages 16–17

A woodland ride in spring

Pages 42–43

A young woodland in the snow

Pages 100–101

*A carpet of Wood Anemones on ancient woodland ground. Note that
there are some Douglas Fir which survived the 1987 hurricane.*

*With thanks to the Estate of James MacGibbon for permission to
reproduce the extract from the poem 'Alone in the Woods' by Stevie
Smith, on page 2.*

The extract on page 2 from The Diversity of Life *by Edward O. Wilson
(Allen Lane, The Penguin Press, 1993) © Edward O. Wilson 1992, is
reproduced by permission of Penguin Books Ltd.*

Extracts from Flora Britannica *by Richard Mabey, published by Sinclair
Stevenson, 1996, are reproduced by permission of Chatto & Windus.*

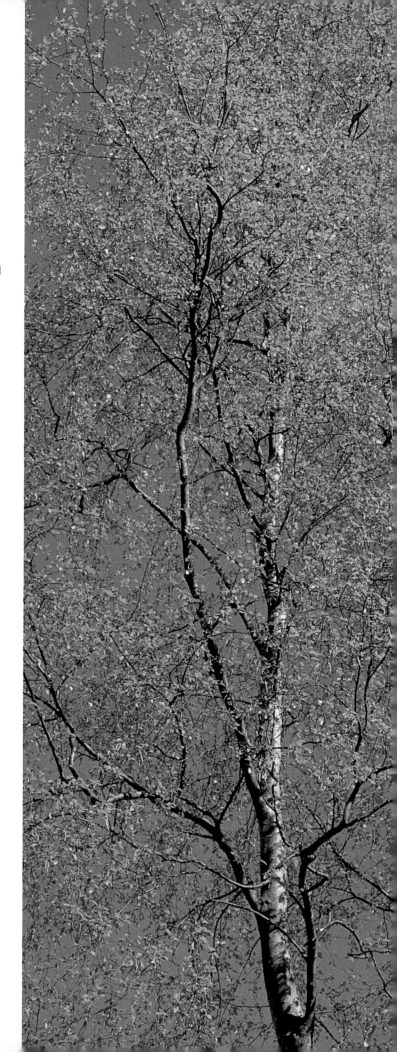

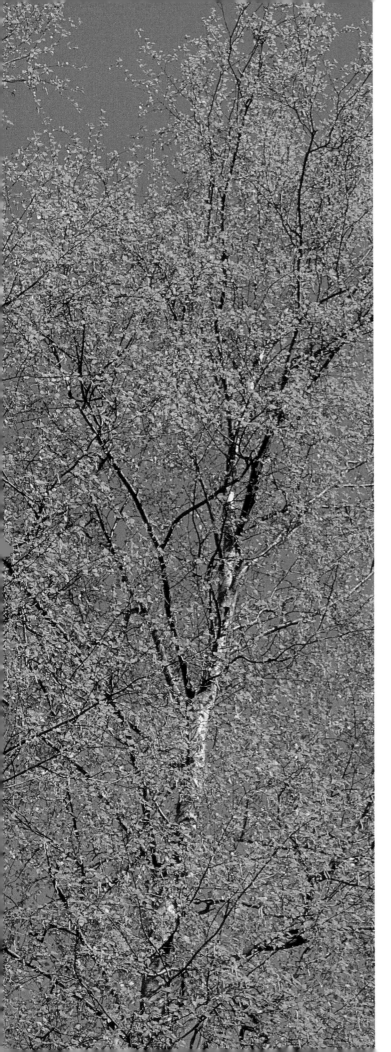

Contents

FOREWORD   7

INTRODUCTION   9

CREATING A WOODLAND   17
Planning a Woodland   18
Propagation, Planting & Protection   22
Community Planting   38

NATIVE TREES AND SHRUBS   43
A Guide to Native Species   44

THE FOREST FLOOR   101
A Guide to Forest Floor Plants   102

CONCLUSION   116

TREE ORGANISATIONS AND SUPPLIERS   118

GLOSSARY   122

BIBLIOGRAPHY   123

INDEX OF PLANTS   124

GENERAL INDEX   127

ACKNOWLEDGEMENTS   128

Foreword

In the native woodland world we spend so much time arguing and debating, and walking the fine line between promoting natural processes and encouraging human intervention. So it is nice to see that a practical author has cut right across that debate, and decided for herself just how much intervention is appropriate in ancient woodland management.

Native or 'semi-natural' woodlands are the result of a distinctive combination of centuries of husbandry skills carried out under the name of traditional woodsmanship, matched by an equally long period when the forces of nature have been at work. Ancient woodlands are neither entirely natural, nor are they man-made; they contain the benefits of both approaches. So it is indeed refreshing to read a wholly practical book which steers a nice line between nature and human intervention.

The book aims to help people create high quality natural character woodland, but with some of the planter's own personality captured in the design, and all in a reasonable human timescale! I commend the book to those who will carry out this kind of work themselves, and hope that their lives are enriched by the experience, as well as by the resulting woodland ecosystem, which will continue to mature, and will then outlive us all.

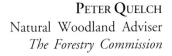

PETER QUELCH
Natural Woodland Adviser
The Forestry Commission

Photograph by Eric Herbert

Introduction

Trees, whether growing in tropical forests, deserts or temperate climes, have always had a special fascination for me. For nearly forty years I have grown and nurtured trees in the garden and in the wild. It was not, however, until after the 1987 hurricane that the subject of native woodlands gripped me. I was the immeasurably fortunate owner of forty acres, mostly woodland, much of which consisted of 'cash' trees such as Douglas Fir (*Pseudotsuga menziesii*), which came down like dominoes in the storm. The trauma of fallen trees everywhere, round the house and blocking access, turned into a miracle. The seemingly barren coniferous earth had once been ancient woodland, and when cleared and replanted with only native species, it underwent a complete transformation. That miracle was the inspiration for this book.

You may not be able to plant trees on ancient woodland sites, but you can and should recreate them for yourself and the future.

About trees

Writers, poets, artists and musicians have, for millennia, been inspired by forests and individual trees. Indeed, we ordinary mortals have all at some time been struck with awe and amazement at the sheer majesty and magnificence of trees. The wonderful shimmering grey-green of tall Beeches can be breathtaking, and ancient Oaks seem to have a gnarled wisdom all their own. There is something magical and mystical about trees and about primeval forests.

But trees are far more than just founts of inspiration; they were and are an integral part of human evolution. They are a source of food, energy and shelter. The weapons for early wars were fashioned out of wood. The first wheel, considered a major landmark in modern development, was made from wood. Early ships, without which extensive trade, communications and colonisation of the globe would not have been possible, were made from wood. The paper for books and journals – indispensable sources of learning – was made from wood. One could write *ad infinitum* about the myriad uses of trees and how they have affected humankind.

Until *homo sapiens* began to clear land for farming and husbandry, trees covered a large part of the globe. Millennia later the agricultural revolution was followed by the industrial, and from then on, spiralling populations made ever-increasing demands on wood.

Woodlands now have to contend with acid rain and the vagaries of weather caused by global warming. It is a wonder that any trees have survived under these immense pressures. Many individuals and certainly commercial corporations treat forests as bottomless resources, oblivious to the miracles they generate all around us.

Wherever there are forests, the climate is tempered and there will be precious rain and water. Woodlands support over

Opposite

In the Woods
by Asher B. Durand

Artists through the ages have been inspired by trees. This painting captures the mystery and magic of a primeval forest.

9

seventy-five percent of our planet's amazing biodiversity. Today, trees, if present in sufficient numbers, could also rid the world of much pollution.

The few individuals who foresaw, at least in some measure, what was bound to happen, were not exactly ignored, but then, like now, commercial considerations prevailed. In Tudor times, the height of the wooden shipbuilding industry, attempts were made to protect the forests. In the Statute of Woods of 1543, owners' rights to fell timber were restricted and they were ordered to replant trees to 'cure the spoils and devastations that have been made in the woods'.

John Evelyn, diarist, author and garden designer, published his *Sylva or A Discourse of Forest-Trees* in 1664 as a protest against the destruction of trees for use by iron foundries and glass factories.

There might have been small pauses in the relentless destruction, but trees continued to be seen as an expendable commodity rather than as living entities deserving nurture and respect.

In the early part of the twentieth century, necessity forced some replanting, but sadly most of this was done for cash crops, with the result that one could see vast tracts of one-species forests, consisting mainly of fast-growing conifers, that gave little or no consideration to other forms of wildlife. Indeed, a walk through one of these 'forests' was singularly depressing: the dark, gloomy forest floor, totally devoid of vegetation, was silent and with no signs of wildlife. Some organisms survived, but often of the virulent kind, multiplying at inconceivable rates when faced with such an unending supply of food. The plagues of pests produced by this one-species planting encouraged the use of chemical pesticides.

Such environmental mismanagement was not, of course, confined to Britain. All around the world, people have cleared land to replant the same cash-generating trees and plants, forcing many species near to extinction, whilst on the other hand failing to exploit the possibilities of relatively unknown species. The destruction of trees has had catastrophic consequences in many parts of the world: we would do well to remember that deserts like the Sahara once flourished with trees (and could do so again). Yet, as I write, we are felling trees globally ten times faster than they can regenerate.

By the end of the twentieth century, farming and industry had depleted forests out of all recognition, and in Britain mere ghostly remnants of primeval forests and natural woodlands remained – only about one percent!

By this time, though, there was a groundswell of public awareness of ecology and conservation: plants, insects, birds, mammals, indeed all living organisms were at last perceived as part of a huge interlocking chain. Species of plants, animals and birds were becoming extinct at an alarming rate. It became obvious that if any kind of biodiversity, or indeed whole ecosystems, were to be preserved, a totally holistic approach to conservation was essential. It was no good stopping the hunting of birds or predation of their eggs, without also preserving and re-creating their habitats; or growing buddleias and stonecrops to attract butterflies, without also growing the food plant for the larvae.

Organisations sprang up everywhere, desperately trying to save tracts of 'natural' land from those intent on more and more houses, roads and factories. With meagre

This Scots Pine, in a remnant of a primeval forest in Scotland, is between three and four hundred years old.

11

Apart from a few surviving young Oaks, this land was part of a solid plantation of Douglas Fir (Pseudotsuga menziesii) under whose canopy virtually no woodland plants grew. The 1987 hurricane flattened all the conifers. The area was cleared, leaving only the stumps, and replanted solely with native trees and shrubs, aided by a grant from the Forestry Commission. Within a year the area was teeming with ancient woodland plants.

The area would have been an ideal candidate for natural regeneration, without human intervention, but this would take many decades, and it would not have the diversity now present after only a few years. Without careful management, it would have been a Birch thicket for half a century or more.

Natural woodlands

What exactly is a 'natural woodland'? The phrase conjures up different images to different people. To some it means ancient or primeval forests that have evolved over centuries with no human intervention. Sadly, very few of these remain in Europe or North America, and virtually none in Britain. Even the vast tracts of forest that can be seen (especially from a plane) in, say, New England or Canada, are mostly secondary or even tertiary growths – that is, the original forest was cut down and regrew either once or twice. The colonists and early settlers somehow managed to fell almost everything in sight – an incredible feat considering the millions of hectares involved and the fact that they had no modern machinery.

Others think of a natural woodland as one where an area of ground is allowed to develop naturally, without human intervention. In this case it is true that, in sixty to a hundred years 'something' will have grown, but unless the land was previously, or is adjacent to, natural woodlands, this approach is unlikely to succeed. What grows will probably be neither indigenous nor particularly natural, nor will it contain the diversity of flora and fauna that was once there.

In many parts of the world the introduction of foreign species is wreaking havoc among the native flora and fauna, and this is particularly true of the British Isles. For several centuries, far too many species have been imported and cultivated, culminating with the intrepid Victorian botanists, such as Douglas, Wilson and others, who brought to Britain plants from almost every corner of the world. Although many of these

financial resources, they have acquired pockets of natural land which they preserve, manage and maintain. More importantly, in the twenty-first century they are educating and mustering public opinion. 'People power' is becoming a formidable weapon for holding politicians, developers and corporations in check.

However, we have to go one step further. Organisations such as the Woodland Trust, Wildlife Trusts, Plant Life, and many more can educate people and protect and nurture the land they acquire. However, this land is still only a tiny percentage – most is still privately owned. If landowners, farmers, and anyone possessing a garden, large or small, devoted at least some of it to planting native trees and shrubs, many of our flora and fauna could be brought back from the brink of extinction, and much of our biodiversity could be regained.

A wonderful step in the right direction has been community planting of natural woodlands – a sight inconceivable until quite recently.

plants are wonderful and beautiful, the practice can have disastrous results. In Britain, a piece of ground left to grow 'naturally' could well end up being taken over by rhododendrons (*Rhododendron ponticum*), laurels (*Prunus laurocerasus*) or Japanese knotweed (*Polygonum cuspidatum*), none of which are native. If the soil has been impoverished by the use of chemicals, the result could well be just scrub or dense areas of bracken (*Pteridium aquilinum*).

George F. Peterken in his book *Natural Woodland* speculates what might happen if people suddenly deserted our island and nature was allowed to take over. He reckons the results would not be very different from those I have described, except that the non-native Sycamore (*Acer pseudoplatanus*) would be a first class contender for a 'take-over'.

The same is true of the importation of animals and insects out of their natural habitats. The existence of certain pests is another reason why non-intervention in a native, natural woodland may not succeed. The main culprits are deer (some imported), rabbits (imported), grey squirrels (also imported) and other rodents. The delicate natural balance, which nature strives to maintain, has been so disturbed that these animals are proliferating out of all proportion to available habitats and making short shrift of any unprotected plants. Attempts are being made to bring back birds of prey, which might redress the balance, but inevitably progress is slow. Yet we do everything to try and exterminate the native fox, which preys on some of these pests! The wolf, that wonderful creature, so unjustly maligned over centuries, has long been extinct in Britain. Moves are being made by some environmentalists to

reintroduce it, which might result in a more natural balance. I hope they succeed, but they will have many battles trying to overcome centuries of prejudice from farmers and the general public alike.

Currently scientists are carefully monitoring the Asian Gypsy Moth, which appeared here in the 1990s, and which could pose a serious threat to hundreds of species of plants, especially in warm, dry conditions. The same is true of the handsome Asian Longhorn Beetle (black with white spots).

Furthermore, we are facing climatic changes which mean that some protective measures are vital if planting is to succeed. The effects of a rise in temperature are to some extent predictable, but the vagaries of extreme winds, storms, floods and drought are not. Extreme winds will devastate large trees, and floods can sweep away everything in their path. Severe droughts destroy most young plants, if careful management is not used to reduce their effects. Most native species can withstand any amount of cold at the right time in winter, but mild winters followed

Part of the same area pictured opposite eight years later. In the background are a few of the surviving Oaks. Each year the forest floor produces an abundance of anemones, bluebells, campions and other woodland flowers – so long as the brambles and Birch saplings are kept to a minimum.

An interpretation of a native woodland by machine embroiderer, Alison Holt.

by late severe frosts can be disastrous, and Britain seems to be experiencing this phenomenon more frequently now. When one hears of snow and hail in Saudi Arabia, anything seems possible anywhere!

The future

What is the answer? Obviously, something should be done, but inevitably opinions will differ as to how it can be achieved. Many will claim that trees or other wild flora should only be planted in their original habitat; others believe that once planted, nature should take its course. Compromise seems the answer – it is no good arguing about the best way, during which time more species will have become extinct. Judicious replanting of woodlands followed by sensitive management can recreate and extend some of our lost natural woodlands and ecosystems. With some management, trees and shrubs are more likely to survive

and grow more quickly, as also many of our native wild flowers, mosses, lichens, grasses and fungi, and with them the birds, butterflies, insects and reptiles that rely on woodlands and verges. Many of these are hurtling towards extinction, so time is paramount.

We cannot know all the plants that once grew in a particular area of land that has since been farmed or urbanised for centuries. It is worth trying, as far as possible, to find out what was native to the area, but if you are tempted to grow something that was apparently not indigenous, I can see no harm in attempting to do this. Unless you completely change the soil, which is impossible, or create a totally artificial environment, the plants will decide whether they will grow and thrive there or not.

I hope by now the purpose of this book is clear. If you are a farmer, have a garden, own some land, or are considering what to do with an area of park land or school grounds, give some thought to devoting part of it to replanting with native species. Even a few square metres can support some trees and shrubs and with them an astonishing variety of wild flowers and wildlife. If possible, choose only true native species - it is those which support our biodiversity rather than the many imports, even if they have been with us a long time. Also, do not think: 'but I shall never see any real results in my lifetime'. I hope to show that extraordinary results can be achieved in a very few years. Moreover, there is nothing more satisfying or fulfilling than watching a seed or minute plant grow year by year into something beautiful and substantial. Also heed well the warning and appeal by John Evelyn over three hundred years ago in his *Sylva,* and think of the poverty of future generations without the amazing and bewildering biodiversity of life:

'We would address ourselves to our better natured Countrymen that such woods as do yet remain intire, might be carefully Preserved, and such as are Destroyed, sedulously repaired. For I observe there is no part of Husbandry, which man commonly more Fail in, neglect, and have cause to repent of, than that they did not begin Planting betimes, without which they can expect neither Fruit, Ornament, or Delight from their labours.'

About this book

The first part of the book gives guidance on planning both large and small woodlands. The great importance of rides, glades and ponds is also covered. Thereafter the book gives totally practical advice on how to plant, maintain and manage your woodland with minimal intervention and yet cope with weeds, pests, diseases and the effects of drought. There is also a section on community planting by my friend, Andrew Beer, who works for the Woodland Trust.

The second part contains information, with illustrations, of all the native trees and shrubs that once covered most of Britain. This may sound formidable, but there are in fact fewer than a hundred species and only thirty-three of these are trees.

Photographs have been used instead of detailed descriptions of the plants. Although I have sometimes given the former and current uses of the wood, the book is in no way intended for commercial timber production nor even for sustainable woodlands. Apart from minimal management, the woodlands should be left to evolve naturally for the enjoyment of future generations.

Finally there is a section devoted to augmenting the existing wild plants on the forest floor. I cover only a selection of the hundreds of possibilities, and again I have kept to native wild species. The bibliography also includes some standard reference works on wild flowers. There is also a section of helpful organisations and suppliers of trees, shrubs and wild flowers (both seeds and plants), all of which were in existence at the time of going to press.

The book makes no pretence of being academic, but attempts to be totally pragmatic.

These days there is plenty of advice available on how to produce a garden full of spectacular imported hybrids. Having read this book, however, I hope you will be inspired to create a natural woodland and discover just how beautiful and fascinating this can be.

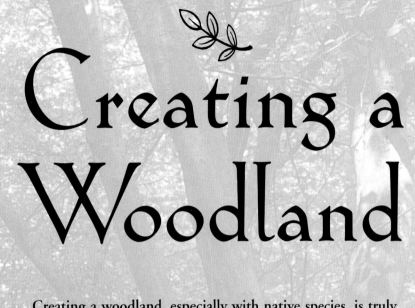

Creating a Woodland

Creating a woodland, especially with native species, is truly fascinating: nurturing the plants, observing the first flowers and fruits, which may coincide with the advent of wildlife not hitherto present, and seeing the first steps in self-generation. In as little as eight to ten years, a healthy woodland will produce a canopy that thins out grasses and undesirable weeds, and a suitable climate for the introduction of many true woodland plants.

Ideally, a new woodland should be planted adjoining an existing one, preferably one consisting of native plants. The reasons are important. Many plants and animals have to 'travel', but cannot make the leap from one patch of woodland to another, even one close by. If you are a group considering purchasing land, or the owner of a considerable acreage, do everything possible to put the new woodland alongside an existing one, since this is the best way to preserve and increase precious biodiversity.

Planning a Woodland

Planning a woodland can be as simple or as complicated as you care to make it. You can be meticulous and scientific, researching all the trees, shrubs and flowers from all angles, including those that were particularly indigenous to your area. Alternatively, you can plant everything haphazardly which is, after all, what nature would do in the self-creation of a woodland. However, this would probably take a century or two to mature, and even then it may not work in present day circumstances. Such a woodland could become dominated by invasive importations, and not display the wonderful biodiversity which is characteristic of a native woodland and which can be achieved by deliberate planting. In practice, therefore, it is best to make some sort of plan.

The second section (pages 43–99) should give you some idea of what native trees and shrubs are available, what they look like and how tall they grow. The latter is important: the tallest should obviously go in the centre, and then fan out with smaller trees and shrubs in intermediate areas and verges. *Euonymous europaeus* (Spindle Tree) would be truly forlorn and grow horribly spindly amidst towering Oaks, Ashes and Beeches! Again, in natural evolvement, this is probably what would occur, but it could take decades, even centuries, for the plant to find a place with sufficient space and light to grow to maturity.

Soil and ground conditions are important. Extremely wet places are probably only suitable for trees such as Alders, Willows and Downy Birch, whereas dry, well-drained areas would be better for Beech and Oak. If care is taken, most trees will grow almost anywhere, but obviously plants such as Elms will grow faster and better on limestone than on heavy clay, and acid-loving ones will do better there than on limestone. Soil preferences, where applicable, are given in the Native Trees and Shrubs section on pages 43–99.

You should also consider carefully where and how you plant trees that eventually form a dense canopy. Relatively little will grow under mature Beech and Hornbeam if closely planted in one place. Nothing at all will grow under dense Holly, Juniper and Yew or even Privet. Unless you are trying to grow a stand of a single species, it is, therefore, best to judiciously space out these plants.

A tiny woodland

If only a few square metres are available, maybe at the bottom of a garden, choose the species with great care. Visualising big native trees in your mind can be very different to the reality, so go and look at some mature specimens. All too often, massive trees are planted in the wrong place, having nowhere

A ride in an ancient woodland site in autumn, believed to be an old drover's road. The trees are mainly Birch, Wild Cherry, Hornbeam and Oak. The ground is densely colonised by bluebells. Strictly speaking, this ride should be widened, but it has been left as it is, because the banks contain many mosses and lichens.

to spread and sometimes causing future neighbour disputes. However, a few stalwarts such as Oak and Beech, given sufficient space and a well-chosen forest floor (see page 101) can make a very lovely 'woodland', buzzing with wildlife. Alternatively you can opt for the smaller natives such as Spindle, Crab Apple, Buckthorn and some of the Sorbus family, interspersed with Holly or Juniper. Such a woodland would not only look pretty all year round, but would also provide food and shelter for many birds and insects.

A large woodland

A site of one, two or more acres is large enough to plant a good mixture of trees and shrubs of all sizes. Estimate the number of each species required which will, of course, depend on how closely they are planted. You can plant as closely as one metre apart, or three or four. In the former case, extensive thinning will be required within a few years, unless many do not survive. Even if planted four metres apart, some thinning will be necessary if the trees are to display their full splendour in maturity. Avoid planting trees in straight lines, and keep the outer edges ragged. If you intend 'mowing' the weeds, allow sufficient space for machinery. Whatever you do, nature will in time take its course, and it is a matter of choice how much human intervention takes place.

RIDES AND GLADES

Rides and glades – open paths and spaces – are paramount in any woodland, even in a small one of an acre or two, if any sort of biodiversity is going to be achieved. It is important that these be included at the outset. They are essential for both plants, birds, invertebrates and much more.

Many woodland plants will grow in the shade of the canopy, and flower before it comes into full leaf. Many more grow wherever sunlight can penetrate. Plants that would normally grow in now scarce meadows or unimproved grasslands will flourish in rides and glades in summer and autumn. Whilst the larvae of many moths and butterflies find food in the trees, the

butterflies themselves require the nectar and pollen of summer flowers. Some birds even prefer open sites for nesting. Plants such as dandelions and thistles provide seeds for finches. In fact, trees and open spaces together can support some three quarters of Britain's flora and fauna.

Here are some things to remember about rides and glades:
• Plant only small trees and shrubs at the edge of rides and glades.
• Initially rides should be at least 5–6m (16–20ft), preferably more. Once trees reach 20 or 30m (65–98ft), the rides should be at least as wide.
• Care should be taken that thick grass or invasive plants such as Bracken do not take over to the exclusion of all else.
• If you are lucky, wild native plants will introduce themselves both under the canopy

Above: A wet woodland verge in a nature reserve dominated by Cirsium vulgare *(Spear Thistle), and various Sedges, (Carex spp). Note the tall Marsh Thistle (C. palustre) in the background.*

A well-proportioned ride in an ancient woodland where Beeches dominate. Note the 'cut' path in the centre, higher vegetation further out and finally shrubs.

and in the sunny spaces. The number and variety will depend on neighbouring vegetation. If woodlands, coppices or hedges are present, you should get a goodly selection. If not, some may have to be introduced (see page 101).

• Outer shrubs may have to be pruned back or coppiced every 10–15 years.

• Prune or coppice when plants are still dormant, usually October to January.

• North/south rides will produce different vegetation from east/west ones, and micro-climates can be encouraged by keeping edges ragged.

• If introducing plants, do not force them to grow by any artificial means (fertilizers and chemicals) just because you like them, nor swamp the available space with just one or two species. If you have done everything right and a plant still will not grow (remember wild plants are often more difficult than cultivated ones), it means that neither soil nor conditions are right, in which case it is best to leave well alone.

A very wild pond dominated by Reedmace, (Typhia spp), often called Bullrush.

PONDS

Water in the form of ponds, streams and ditches is essential to all wildlife. So many 'dew' and natural ponds up and down the country have disappeared into agricultural crops, that ponds in any natural area are becoming increasingly important. Furthermore, wildlife will, in future, have to face erratic weather conditions – maybe several years of drought followed by deluges – and a pond could be life-saving.

Here are some good reasons for building a pond:

• Ponds will greatly increase the biodiversity of a woodland.

• Many marginal water-loving plants, as well as water plants, will find a home.

• Toads, frogs and other reptiles, currently decreasing at alarming rates, will find a habitat. Even fish have been known to 'appear', apparently out of nowhere, in a newly-made pond.

• Invertebrates all require water in one form or another. Wild honey bees especially will swarm somewhere close to water, which is essential for them.
• Birds, especially in drought conditions, must find water.
• Ponds will help water-loving trees to survive in drought conditions.

Whilst it is probably not possible to create a wood through which streams and rivers flow, it is quite possible to build a pond or even make do with ditches in the low-lying parts of the plantation. Modern machinery makes short work of digging a pond, so the only constraints would seem to be financial.

Take into account some of the following when building a pond:
• Test the pond site by digging a 1–2m (3–6ft) pit and leave for several winter months. This will give you an idea of the water level. If it does not fill up at all, change the site or be prepared to line it.
• Do not use plastic liners or pre-formed ponds. They are not remotely natural and will only cause problems in the future. If the soil will not hold water, line it with puddling clay, which can be purchased.

• Create a pond *before* any planting takes place and choose the lowest lying ground for the site.
• Soil from the pond can be used to create banks and mounds.
• Avoid choosing a site into which either chemicals or slurry from neighbouring non-organic farms may drain. The water will become polluted and frogs especially are susceptible to this type of pollution.
• Ponds should have several levels: shallow at the edges, deeper ledges and finally the full depth.

In time, the creation and management of rides, glades and ponds will become a science which is, as yet, in its infancy. A great deal is known about all these elements as individual entities, but relatively little about their inter-relationship and interaction. With an abundance of available land, nature would find its own delicate balance between woods, open spaces and water, but in a country where land is so scarce, we have to try to recreate these habitats.

A very small natural pond which reputedly came into existence via a crater made by a V2 bomb in World War II. It is rampant with pond plants and invertebrates, and surrounded by Burr-reeds (Sparganium ssp) and various Sedges (Carex spp).

Propagation, Planting & Protection

PROPAGATION

Once you have a plan of the area to be planted, you have to acquire the selected trees and shrubs. On pages 118–121 there is a list of nurseries specialising in native trees and shrubs and also organisations which should be able to help. You also have to decide whether to buy small, bare-rooted plants or plugs, (or large ones which will cost more) or whether to grow them from seed. Make sure you buy from a reputable nursery; that the plants look strong and healthy, and that they are true native species rather than hybrids or imported specimens. Plants may be only a few centimetres high, but they can shoot up in one season, and a very high percentage should survive and flourish if sufficient care is taken.

Raising trees and shrubs from seed can be difficult and often results in disappointment. Seed germination is erratic and can be a lengthy business taking many months or even years. Unless you have some experience in raising trees from seed, it may be better to buy small plants.

Propagation from fresh seed

The best way to propagate trees and shrubs is from fresh seeds collected as soon as they ripen in late summer. Try to obtain seeds from an existing natural woodland as there will be less chance of ending up with a collection of hybrids. Permission should always be sought from the owners, but they are unlikely to refuse it. On no account uproot or damage any trees or plants. Put seeds in separate bags and label them.

In many cases, better results can be obtained if you subject the seeds to periods of cold and warm stratification (see glossary). Cold and warm stratification are designed to imitate the natural process in which the wild seeds are scattered and then lie dormant in the ground all winter, subjected to cold, frost and wind. As the soil warms in the spring and conditions are right, they may germinate.

Cold stratification should be carried out in normal outside temperatures. For subsequent warm stratification, the boxes should be moved into a dark room with a temperature of 15–18ºC. The approximate periods of stratification are given under the individual plants. As soon as seedlings emerge, move into light and then pot on.

Some tough seeds require scarification with emery paper before sowing. Information is given under the individual plants.

Fresh seeds with outer fleshy casings, such as Hawthorn and Cherry, require maceration, that is removing the outer casing

The three seed boxes below illustrate the erratic germination of trees and shrubs. Left: Hawthorn (Crataegus monogyma) of which only a very small percentage has germinated. Others might germinate the following year. Centre: Field Maple (Acer campestre) with a reasonable percentage of germination. Right: Privet (Ligustrum vulgare) which is growing in abundance! Seeds, whether in pots, boxes or beds, should be covered with sand or grit and kept moist until the seedlings emerge.

and extracting the seeds without damaging them. Small quantities can be done by hand.

Fresh seeds can also be sown directly into the ground of a designated woodland. Put several seeds where you would normally plant a seedling and cover lightly.

Theoretically, this method should be like natural self-generation. In practice it does not necessarily work. Wild plants can be stubborn and will only germinate in a site of their own choosing. In nature, thousands – maybe millions – of seeds are dispersed, but only a small percentage will germinate.

Propagation from purchased seeds

All purchased seeds will have been dried, and it is even more important to cold and/or warm stratify them. Details are given under individual plants. Cold stratification can also be done by mixing the seed with moist sand or perlite and putting them in labelled plastic bags in a refrigerator (not the freezer compartment). The optimum temperature is 1–5ºC. Inspect the seeds every week or so. If you see tiny roots emerging, sow immediately.

Sowing

Sow the seeds immediately and as evenly as possible into pots, boxes or beds. The medium used should be well-draining, i.e. a good mixture of soil, leaf mould or coir and/ or compost. Press in seeds firmly and cover with sand or grit. Tiny seeds only require

pressing into the soil: large ones should be covered by their own depth. The boxes or beds must be kept moist at all times. Seedlings should emerge the following spring, although it may take another year or more for some of the seeds to germinate. As soon as they are large enough to handle, pot on seedlings into small pots or containers.

A small collection of potted on seedlings all grown from seed. Front row: Scots Pine (Pinus sylvestris); middle row: Hornbeam (Carpinus betulus); back row: Ash (Fraxinus excelsior). These would by no means populate a woodland, but are shown solely as an example. Note the use of recycled pots – cream, yoghurt etc.

Propagation from cuttings

A good way of reproducing any plant is by taking cuttings. Nearby woodlands and coppices are bound to have some native trees and shrubs, and taking a number of cuttings will do no harm to the parent plant, providing you only take small cuttings. Always obtain permission from the owners. Cuttings have the added advantage that an exact 'clone' of the parent plant will be reproduced rather than a hybrid from cross-fertilization. Like seeds, cuttings from trees and shrubs can be very temperamental, so do not be disappointed if they do not strike.

Here are some guiding principles for taking cuttings:
• Cuttings should be about 10–20cm (4–8in) and cut with a sharp knife or secateurs at an angle above a bud, and straight at the bottom (an aid to identifying top from bottom when planting).
• Only take cuttings from healthy plants.
• Take 'tip' cuttings, i.e. from the top of a branch, as these will make better shaped plants.
• Take softwood cuttings from spring to early summer.
• Strip all but top leaves, which, if large, can be cut in half to reduce transpiration.
• Cuttings are best taken in early morning when humidity is high and temperatures low.
• Dipping the cuttings into a seaweed root dip can help.
• Small quantities can be planted in pots, but large numbers should be planted in boxes or an outdoor bed.
• Outdoor beds should be prepared in a semi-shaded position (or provide shade by adding a covering such as fleece), cleared of all weeds and covered with 10–15cm (4–6in) of a free-draining, light medium such as sand or grit. Moisture must be maintained at all times by covering with white or clear polythene, or glass.
• Cuttings should be firmly pressed into beds or pots, leaving about two-thirds exposed, and planted 5–8cm (2–3in) apart.
• Hardwood cuttings should be taken in autumn or early winter (as soon as the plant becomes dormant). Cut off any soft wood, and either plant immediately or make bundles and store in a cool place in labelled buckets containing moist sand. Plant out in pots, boxes or beds in early spring.
• It is possible to buy plugs/root trainers which are made specially for cuttings, and have the added advantage that you can inspect them for emerging roots.

The time it takes for cuttings to strike and the percentage success rate varies enormously from plant to plant. Some trees, such as Willow, will grow whatever you do. A large branch stuck into the open ground will take root! Others, such as Beech, are almost impossible to strike.

An outdoor bed of hardwood cuttings: Dogwood (Cornus sanguinea). They were planted in spring and had rooted by June.

A small number of cuttings can be planted in a pot with an inflated plastic bag secured over the top to retain moisture.

PLANTING

It is a good idea to mark the position of each tree or shrub before embarking on planting. There are three ways of planting seedlings and saplings: heeling in, root ball and digging in. Planting should either be done before Christmas, or in January, February or March. Most foresters prefer January. Early planting is essential to give the plants time to develop good roots before the drier weather sets in. March may be a little late, especially in southern areas, unless you are prepared to water individually and regularly.

The following sections on weeds and pests should be read before planting and at least some of the protective measures discussed on page 28 onwards should be taken at the same time as planting.

Heeling in

This is really the only method of planting up a large area reasonably quickly – see the demonstration below. A small trench can also be dug and seedlings inserted and firmed in.

If you are going to use protective measures, do so immediately, as these small plants can disappear in one night! Any type of tree shelter or wire netting can be used (see pages 30–31).

A bundle of bare-rooted seedlings – in this case Hazel (Corylus avellana) – as they arrive from the nursery. Plant out immediately. If this is not possible, heel in the whole bundle into soil and keep watered. The success rate will be small if seedlings are allowed to dry out. If using tree shelters or guards, insert over the top of the seedling, taking care not to damage the branches.

Drive the spade into the ground at an angle.

Move the spade back towards you, thus creating a small hole/slit.

Insert the seedling and firm back the soil.

Give the seedling a good 'tug' to ensure it is firmly in the ground.

Pendunculate Oak (Quercus robur) self-sown seedling.

The above seedling and those on the following two pages are all self-generated. They will do this in the right circumstances but rarely in thick grass, bracken or areas densely covered in 'weeds' such as brambles.

Root ball

Larger plants can be purchased in the form of root balls, that is with hessian or sacking and soil tied round the roots. Make sure the sacking is fully biodegradable. Dig a hole the exact size of the root ball and firm in. Although more expensive, root ball planting increases the chances of survival, and good results are quickly obtained. However, having spent the extra money, it is even more important to protect the trees against deer and rodents, weeds and drought (see pages 28–35).

You may find it difficult to insert a tube or shelter without either disturbing the root system of root balls or pot-grown plants, or damaging any extensive outer branches. If this is the case, either make your own protection with netting (see pages 30–31) or use one of the plastic spiral shelters which can be wound round the trunk (see page 30.)

Self-sown Ash (Fraxinus excelsior) seedling.

Self-sown Field Maple (Acer campestre) seedling.

Mark out piece of ground the same size as the root ball.

Dig a hole to fit the root ball.

Lift up topsoil and/or turf.

Plant the root ball and firm in, making sure the soil does not come above the base of the tree.

Digging in

Pot-grown specimens of trees can be purchased. These are expensive, and 'digging in' is time-consuming, but will be of enormous benefit to the plant in the long run. Dig a fair-sized hole, mix any kind of compost/humus with soil, and plant the seedling or sapling. Firm down well with your feet. Some experts do not approve of compost or humus being used for wild native plants. However, in areas susceptible to many rainless weeks or months, these additions will give the sapling a much better chance of survival.

Seedlings and saplings should be planted 1–4m (3–13ft) apart.

The addition of tree mats or spats, or plain *wet* newspaper covered by any kind of mulch or wood chips, will retain moisture in the soil for several months and help give the tree/shrub a really good start (see pages 28 and 33). Do not forget to remove the non-biodegradable mats or plastic.

Self-sown Beech (Fagus sylvatica) seedling.

Carefully insert the sapling into the hole. Mix compost or humus with the soil.

Self-sown Silver Birch (Betula pendula) seedling.

Dig a hole as for root balls, somewhat larger than the size of the pot. If the ground is at all dry, the hole should be watered well. Carefully take the sapling out of the pot and slightly knead the sides to loosen the roots.

Make sure that the base of the sapling is not covered by soil and/or compost. Firm in well.

PROTECTION

In theory and in ideal circumstances, one should be able to leave woodland species to their own devices once planted. However, if you do this, the survival rate of individual plants and the chances of a successful woodland will probably be very small. Plants are threatened by three main enemies: weeds, pests and drought, and also by various diseases and disorders.

Weeds

Most weeds will probably not actually kill a plant, but if they are allowed to grow totally unchecked around the roots, the plant's growth rate will be very slow. Weeds, especially grass, compete fiercely for all the nutrients and water in the soil. The one sure

A collection of manufactured tree mats and spats. All must be anchored with pegs (often provided) or rocks. Most are made of permeable plastic, which are better as they let water through (the top two are not permeable). The two beige ones at the bottom are made from biodegradable jute. There are many varieties on the market, but purchasing purpose-made tree mats or spats can be costly.

way of keeping weeds at bay long enough for the trees to become well established (maybe several years) is by the sheer hard work of hoeing and weeding by hand. Strimming and mowing are also an option, but great care should be taken not to damage the plants. However, there are also steps you can take which will ease the work and reduce the time you have to spend.

• A good mulch of compost, leaf mould, bark or wood chips or shreddings round the plant will not only suppress weeds, but also retain moisture. A layer of wet newspaper or cardboard underneath the mulch will keep the weeds at bay even longer and retain more moisture. Both will eventually rot into the ground.

• Other suitable weed-suppressing mulches are spoiled hay, straw or grass mowings. An unusual mulch can be made from sheep fleeces which take a long time to rot. This may sound fanciful, but farmers are paid so little for the fleeces that they are often willing to dispose of them, added to which only white fleeces can be sold to the wool board. Black and brown ones look very good on the ground!

• A tree mat or tree spats placed round the base of the plant will suppress weeds. There are quite a number on the market made of different materials, but if large quantities are involved, it can be expensive.

• Plastic can also be anchored round the base of the plant and is very much cheaper than tree mats or spats.

• Do not forget to remove both plastic and any kind of non-degradable mats as soon as they show any signs of deteriorating, or the tree has outgrown them.

• Many people will advocate the use of herbicides round young trees. Of course, this is far less time-consuming, but herbicides are a contradiction in a natural woodland. Careless spraying might kill not only the tree you are trying to protect, but also potential wild flowers and other plants. Chemicals are also detrimental or even poisonous to animals, birds and insects, thus negating all attempts at restoring biodiversity.

• Grass, especially couch grass (*Agropyron repens*), is the most destructive and widespread 'weed'. Cutting or strimming will only make it grow thicker. Suppression or hand weeding is the only answer.

• Bracken (*Pteridium aquilinum*) can be very invasive and destructive. I have areas of woodland that were flattened by the 1987 hurricane; and the small patches of Bracken that had been present were suddenly given unlimited access to light. They spread at an alarming rate, smothering everything by late spring so that only a small percentage of the trees planted survived. They also inhibit self-generation later on. Regular cutting or strimming is effective. Do this before the fronds uncurl and again in the late summer before the spores ripen. If this is repeated for several years, the Bracken will weaken or disappear.

• Brambles (*Rubus fructicosus*) are great for hedgerows, where the fruits are appreciated by people, birds and animals alike. In a woodland their use is limited. Once a good canopy forms, they do not grow tall, but thickly and fruitlessly cover the ground and exclude light from many potential woodland flowers. They also tend to strangle self-generating trees and shrubs, with the exception of Oaks. On the other hand, they do afford protection and nesting sites for a number of woodland birds. A good balance should, therefore, be maintained. Manual weeding is, of course, best but very labour-intensive. It is almost impossible to get out all the roots, but at least cut off the 'crown' which shoots out many branches. Cutting and strimming will keep Brambles down, but will ultimately make them proliferate. Brambles send out two, three or more stolons (runners) every year. If they are just cut rather than pulled out, there will be three or four plants the following year where previously there was only one!

• Birch seedlings and saplings can be a great nuisance, but they usually only occur in vast numbers where there was once a natural woodland. Unfortunately, pulling them up by the roots is the only option – cutting will only serve to coppice this vigorous, hardy tree. Once a canopy forms, they thin out naturally, but give them a chink of light and they will take over!

• Whilst the trees and shrubs are small, care must be taken that they are not literally strangled by some of our more vigorous climbers. These include Honeysuckle, Black Bryony, wild Roses and sometimes Ivy. All are very attractive and welcome once the tree can take care of itself.

• If possible, avoid uprooting wild flowers whilst assiduously weeding!

• Trees will self-generate in as little as five to ten years, but they will only do so if they can get sufficient light.

Left: An unusual mulch of fleece, which, if used with paper underneath, is not only an effective weed supressor, but also a good moisture retainer.

Below: Bracken (Pteridium aquilinum) only a few centimetres tall in the middle of summer. It had been strimmed twice the previous year. It almost disappeared in the third year.

Bottom: Bramble (Rubus fructicosus) showing at least four new plants (stolons) from a single stem.

29

Pests

Right: Trees planted with tree shelters for protection.

Below: A collection of tree guards. You can make your own with wire netting, or purchase various solid plastic, meshed or spiral ones which will expand as the tree grows. Nearly all have to be staked and tied, but follow the manufacturers' instructions.

The pests most likely to damage young trees and shrubs are rabbits, squirrels and other rodents, and deer. Curiously, none of these seem to attack self-sown seedlings – most survive, yet unprotected planted ones disappear. I have tried transplanting self-sown seedlings into the same environment quite close by, but without exception they were eaten down to the ground.

As yet there seems no good scientific explanation for this phenomenon. We know that plants can develop immunity or resistance to disease and pests. For instance, some trees, if attacked by a pest, can warn

Below: A healthy crop of self-sown Ash seedlings, most of which survived the attention of deer, rabbits and other rodents. They are now one metre tall and should be thinned.

their neighbours, which will produce a repellent. It is possible that forcing a plant to grow in our time and place, rather than the time and place of its choosing, weakens or destroys its defence mechanisms. Whatever the explanation, self-sown plants have a greater survival rate and grow faster and stronger than their transplanted relatives.

The best and cheapest form of protection against rabbits, squirrels, other rodents and deer is provided by the many tree shelters or guards on the market (see left). Amongst the best are those developed by Graham Tuley in the 1970s, sometimes called, 'Tuley tubes' or 'tree tubes' (see also page 33).

Nowadays, tree shelters are made of twin-wall polypropylene and come in various shapes and heights. Experiments tend to show that the best protection is afforded by the tubular ones, since square ones can damage the plant once it emerges by rubbing on the edges in high wind, whereas the flared rim of the round ones do not.

Tree guards are a mesh made from plastic or even metal, and used to protect trees from mammals. However, unlike tree shelters, they do not provide a humid microclimate, so they are only an option in areas guaranteed good, wet summers and winters. Also, side shoots develop through the mesh, making them difficult to remove.

Both shelters and guards require staking. Avoid very soft woods as they tend to rot in two or three years and heavy winds will blow down both shelter and plant. Sweet Chestnut stakes are best.

Neither tree shelters nor plastic tree guards are wholly biodegradable, whatever the manufacturers claim. They begin to break down after a numbers of years, sometimes into irritating small pieces which have to be collected. They are best removed before this happens by slitting them with a sharp knife. I have quite a number of shelters that still show no signs of breaking up after twelve years!

The alternative for a large area is fencing. Various estimates and costings have been made as to which is the more economic. There is usually little difference, but fencing is not, in my view, any kind of substitute for individual tree shelters. Fencing will not protect the plants from rabbits (unless dug in), squirrels or other rodents, or against drought.

DEER

Britain has native Roe and Red deer. Fallow deer were probably introduced by the Normans. They are all destructive, but by far the worst 'villains' are two species, both imported, the Muntjac and Sika. The deer population is growing fast, and in some areas has to be culled. Even in relatively suburban gardens deer can be a considerable nuisance.

This Spindle Tree (Euonymous europaeus) was totally decimated by a stag cleaning his antlers. The tree regrew the following year, despite being continually 'nibbled', whilst the neighbouring tree remained totally untouched.

They can decimate a whole tree plantation overnight. If your trees are in any danger from these animals, protect them and save yourself a lot of heartache.

Deer are regular visitors to my woodland but they do not, I am glad to say, include either the Muntjak or Sika. They seem to confine their browsing mainly to Guelder Rose (*Viburnum opulus), Sorbus spp,* and Ash (*Fraxinus excelsior)*, but they have not done a great deal of damage. Quite a number of trees have been irreparably scarred by stags 'cleaning' their antlers in late autumn in preparation for the rutting season. But deer are, after all, as much a part of the natural scene as birds, beetles, caterpillars and fungi, and providing their numbers do not get out of hand and they are allowed some grass grazing in an overcrowded land, they should be welcomed as such. However, you must use tree guards or shelters in the early years! Trees will be protected from deer by shelters 1–1.5m (3–5ft) tall.

Left: Do not allow trees to get into this state. All shelters and guards should be removed as soon as the tree/shrub is large enough to fend for itself. Sometimes the guard itself can damage the tree. They can also be difficult to remove if left on too long.

RABBITS, VOLES AND OTHER RODENTS

Rabbits are not indigenous. Unfortunately, they are totally out of control despite the continued presence of myxomatosis. They are a prime example of an importation upsetting the delicate balance of nature. At the risk of being castigated by all the animal protection societies, I have to admit I have no compunction about having rabbits culled by any humane means possible. They will gnaw the bark of almost all tree and shrub saplings (sometimes even full-grown trees) and small seedlings will be devoured in their entirety. The trees that survive are likely to succumb to stress, disease or drought in future years. Rabbits can also damage or even eradicate many beautiful and increasingly rare species of wild flowers, including orchids.

Even in Victorian times when there was not quite so much pressure on the land, the writer and horticulturist, William Robinson could find 'no redeeming feature' and 'little excuse for the existence' of rabbits. He referred to them as the 'dreaded vermin of the wild gardener' doing 'incalculable injury to young trees alone'.

The only protection against rabbits is to install short tree shelters or guards, or just plain small-meshed wire netting. Both are tedious and time-consuming, but necessary if you want your plants to survive.

SQUIRRELS

The grey squirrel was imported from North America in the 19th century. Unlike the rabbit, it does not attack very young trees, but waits until they are a fair size and well-established and then wreaks untold damage by ripping off the bark from top to bottom, leaving life-long scars on those that survive. The worst sufferers are Beech and Hornbeam. Squirrels also nip off buds and flowers from many trees. Scientists are working on a contraceptive pill for the grey squirrel which would certainly help, although one would not want to entirely eradicate the population of this otherwise engaging and intelligent creature.

Unfortunately there is little you can do about squirrel damage except humanely trap or shoot the squirrels. Never feed them – it will only encourage more to move in and will not lessen the damage they do.

Above: A very time-consuming but perfect guard against rabbits. Note the thick mulch.

Left: A tree showing rodent damage inflicted in its early years. The bark will rarely heal completely and the tree will always be susceptible to other pests and diseases in times of stress.

Drought

Some of our native trees and shrubs and other wild plants may well be driven northwards by global warming; some could disappear altogether. In the meantime, it would be wise to do everything possible to create conditions in which young plants can survive. Many trees and shrubs, once they are well established and have formed a good canopy, will survive a reasonable drought. It is the young plants that must be protected. Here are some steps you can take:

• All the measures against weeds outlined on page 28–29, apply to drought also.
• The more humus and compost, especially leaf mould, that can be dug into the ground before planting, the better. Compost can retain as much as eighty percent water, whereas the most moisture-retentive soil, clay, can only retain about twenty percent. Also, use all the mulches mentioned in the weed section. The thicker the mulch, the better, but care should be taken not to build up mulch directly on the stems.
• Mulches should be applied only on really wet soil.
• Tree spats and plastic mulches will also help retain moisture.
• Rocks or stones round the base of plants will help.
• Small areas of young seedlings can be watered by hand. Do not use roses or sprinklers: they waste water and help weeds as well! Make sure the water gets only to the roots of the plant.
• Only water late in the evening or very early in the morning – never in sunlight when the percentage of evaporation will be very high.
• The existence of ponds, natural or man-made, can help in drought conditions and some of the water can be used for small saplings.

The plastic tree shelters used for protection against animals actually had their origins in creating a 'mini-greenhouse' effect. Graham Tuley originally wrapped polythene round mesh guards, and the modern tree shelter has become an essential weapon against drought. The plant performs transpiration, that is it gives off water, but instead of evaporating into the air, the water is trapped in the shelter and runs down to the

base of the plant. Shelters also create a higher temperature inside, and have less air movement and therefore higher humidity, all of which increase the plant's rate of growth and survival. Trials show that trees planted in tree shelters grow faster and survive better than those that are not. The shelters even provide some protection against very late frosts.

I planted several thousand trees after the 1987 hurricane of which about seventy percent have turned into good sturdy specimens. Some are still weaklings and will probably not survive, others succumbed to late frosts, and others quite simply died or were destroyed by careless strimming. A few were attacked by deer, but most survived. I am convinced that this percentage could not have been achieved without the use of tree shelters: not only did they protect the plants, but they helped them to withstand several very dry post-hurricane summers. The missing thirty or forty percent are being more than made up by self-sown seedlings, some already coming from the planted specimens, the oldest of which are only eleven years old. These self-sown seedlings are growing faster than their parents and survive both drought and pests without the use of shelters.

Left: Rowan (Sorbus aucuparia) in late summer showing signs of drought stress. Although it lost all its leaves prematurely, it was sufficiently established to completely recover the following year.

Below: The addition of wet newspaper underneath a thick mulch will retain moisture for a very long time. This operation should only be carried out when the soil is truly wet. If the plant has no protective tree shelter, make sure the mulch does not lie close on the stem. This may rot the base of the plant.

Diseases and disorders

Above: Powdery mildew on a young self-sown Oak which grew perfectly healthy the following year. Mildew also occurs on mature trees.

It is really best not to worry about diseases and disorders. Most diseases originate from pests, but the subject of their relationship is complex and confusing and it is very easy to misinterpret symptoms. The best defence is to grow really healthy plants by observing as much as possible the guidelines on the previous pages. Healthy trees will not readily succumb to diseases. It is trees that have been damaged by human hands, machinery, pests, drought or other extreme weather conditions that will be prone to diseases.

If a devastating disease such as Dutch Elm disease occurs, there is unfortunately little you can do. In the past, chemicals were thought to be the answer, but often they only aggravated the situation because they did not give natural predators or natural defences a chance to develop, and they simultaneously destroyed many other living plants and organisms.

Right: A Guelder Rose shoot showing curling leaves, the sign of an attack by aphids. Note the hoverfly on the top already anticipating a good meal.

Far right: The underside of a badly infected leaf, also from a Guelder Rose plant.

I was recently in Nova Scotia where some of their native Red Spruce (*Picea rubus*) were slowly dying in great numbers from an attack of a bark beetle. Controversy raged about the best method to deal with it, but chemicals were not even considered an option. The debate centred round cutting and burning, or leave well alone! Curiously many Elms (*Ulmus Spp*) have survived in that area.

You cannot expect wild plants to look smart and manicured. Tatty foliage and eaten leaves, anathema to vegetable and flower gardeners, are all part of the natural scene; their absence denotes a lack of beetles, butterflies and other creatures.

Normally trees and shrubs will survive any but a plague attack from invertebrates. For example, I planted a number of Buckthorn (*Rhamnus cathartica*) and Wayfaring trees (*Viburnum lantana*). In both cases, they were totally defoliated in the first year: the former by the larvae of the Brimstone butterfly, the latter by flea beetle and a minute caterpillar. Both species survived but were not attacked quite as voraciously in subsequent years.

Here are some of the commonest signs of diseases and disorders which might worry you but from which, in most cases, the trees and shrubs will recover and flourish in subsequent years:

• In autumn many plants are attacked by various fungi resulting in rust and mildew. Mildew turns the leaves downy white, whilst rust produces blotches, and the leaves turn brown and drop. Young Oaks are especially

prone to mildew, but the same little plant will usually return healthy the next spring.

• Leaves of new shoots, especially Cherry (*Prunus spp*) and Guelder Rose (*Viburnum opulus*) often curl and eventually drop off. This is a symptom of Peach Curl caused by aphids, who in time will be attacked by their own predators – mainly ladybirds, hoverflies and parasitic wasps.

• In late summer, some trees and shrubs display wilting and browning leaves and the tree often becomes denuded of all leaves. Normally, this is only a sign of drought and is the plant's own method of self-preservation. Instead of performing transpiration, it reserves all the available moisture for its trunk and branches.

• Late spring frosts can cause similar damage. Young buds and leaves blacken and die off. Normally the plant recovers, weeks or even months later, but in some cases saplings may die.

• Ground melting from a very heavy frost makes the soil 'heave', virtually ejecting seedlings from the soil. Firm back as quickly as possible. Frost may also cause canker and splitting of barks, but this is rare.

• Sometimes the crowns of older trees defoliate or turn yellow. Smaller trees can turn yellow or brown and die. There could be many reasons, ranging from a root disorder to complex interactions of both living and non-living factors.

• Strange white, red or brown fruit-like growths appear on trees in spring, especially on Oaks. These are signs of the presence of various gall wasps – the growth is the home for eggs and larvae until the adult wasp emerges.

• Much has been written about the Honey Fungus (*Armillaria mellea*) which, it is said, can destroy whole plantations. The toadstools appear only in autumn, but the real damage is being done by masses of underground rhizomorphs that are very difficult to detect, and which can spread from tree to tree. A commercial plantation or orchard might suffer a virulent attack, but a real infestation is unlikely to occur in a well-balanced mixed woodland. Different species of Honey Fungus are now recognised, one of which is not pathogenic. This is the one most likely to be found on old stumps.

• There are many other fungi that attack trees, of which the most virulent example is Dutch Elm disease and *Phytophthora*, which attacks Alder. Unfortunately there is little you can do about this except let nature take its course.

• Honeysuckles (*Lonicera spp*), Ivies (*Hedera spp*), Briony (*Tamus communis* and *Bryonia dioica*), and similar climbing plants are lovely when flowering on trees large enough to look after themselves. However, saplings can literally be strangulated by these climbers, so inspection and pruning or weeding out is advisable.

• If strimming, avoid damaging barks or trunks, as bacteria and pests can enter through open wounds and cause canker and other diseases. The wounds may heal, but will always leave lesions.

Above: Honey Fungus (Armillaria mellea).

Above left: A gall wasp burr on an Oak in spring. They are usually harmless. In some years they appear in great numbers.

• Bonfires can cause severe scorching to barks and similarly leave trees vulnerable to attacks from all kinds of bacteria, fungi, beetles and other pests. Fires are polluting, a nuisance to neighbours and quite unnecessary inside a woodland. It is much better to leave windblown and dead trees and branches, and other prunings, to compost back into the soil, which will enrich it for future generations of flora.

• Sometimes burrs and bizarre malformations form on woody stems and branches. These are usually harmless and despite them a tree can grow to full maturity. They are often caused by some sort of damage to the tree when young – usually by galls and wasps.

Left: A tree showing severe bonfire damage. The damage will never totally heal and will always leave the tree more susceptible to pests and diseases, so that it will probably never attain a ripe old age.

Above: Pin burrs caused by gall wasps – in this case in an Oak tree.

Opposite: A Beech several centuries old. Note the extraordinary protuberance on the trunk, probably caused by physical damage when the tree was young.

Below: Crown Gall on an ancient English Elm (Ulmus procera).

Below: Excessive bud proliferation on Malus sylvestris. This is genetic and occurred when the tree was very young. It still survives.

Community Planting

by Andrew Beer

WOODS & PEOPLE

You can create a natural woodland entirely on your own, if you are lucky enough to own the land and have the time, energy and enthusiasm. However, to do so is to miss a great opportunity to inspire and educate, not to mention the chance of sharing the workload. Planting trees is a simple and powerful way of gaining the interest of people in the natural environment. You are taking a first step by planting a wood, but by inspiring others you can achieve even more.

In practice, most new woods are created by groups of people working together, often with organisations such as parish councils, charitable trusts or local authorities. A team effort is required to help find the land and raise the necessary funds, as well as to carry out the practical work. If you are working with a group, it is important to reach an agreement about your aims. There are many different types and styles of woodland and unless you agree a common vision, there are likely to be conflicts later on.

A community tree planting in progress

Finding a site for a new woodland is often the hardest part of the process. Selecting a site before approaching the landowner is likely to lead to disappointment. Few farmers have spare land or spare money, so you cannot expect them to offer land for free. You may find a supportive landowner, or you may be able to persuade a local authority to provide some land. However, buying land as and when it becomes available is often the only choice. Try and be as patient and flexible as you can.

The cost of acquiring land can be very daunting, but try not to be deterred. Planting a wood is a fabulous proposition for fundraising. You are offering sponsors the chance to support something that will improve the environment, be visible to everyone and last forever! There are not many projects that offer these kinds of benefits and there are numerous sources of funding support that you can try (see also pages 118–119).

Possible sources of funding:

- Local county, town and parish councils
- Other government bodies
- The Forestry Authority
- The National Lottery
- Local and multi-national companies
- Scottish National Heritage
- Charitable trusts
- Involve the local media
- Organise your own jumble sales, raffles and sponsored events

Photograph: Woodland Trust

The site should be:

- Reasonably accessible to
  visitors

- Free from archaeological
  remains and existing
  ecological interest

- Without too many
  wayleaves or constraints
  (power cables, pipes,
  overhead wires)

- Preferably adjacent to
  existing ancient
  woodland or other
  semi-natural habitats.

CONSULTATION

You do not need permission to plant trees, but there are lots of good reasons to consult people. At the very least, it is a simple courtesy to talk to the immediate neighbours about your proposals. Many people are delighted to have a new woodland planned next door, but they will wish to know that it is happening, how the wood will be maintained and what planting is proposed at an early stage.

You might also need some expert advice. It is important to remember that not every piece of land is suitable for planting trees. A piece of grassland that might be considered untidy and worthless for agriculture could well be home to rare plants and insects. Natural grassland is an even more threatened habitat than woodland, so the last thing you would want to do is cause damage by planting trees. If you are unsure, ask your local Wildlife Trust or conservation group (see pages 118–119). Similarly, trees can cause damage to archaeological remains, so if there are any suspicious looking lumps and bumps, ask an archaeologist. In most cases, places of archaeological interest can be incorporated within a woodland design as meadows or glades.

Once you have been inspired by the idea of a new woodland, it is easy to forget that other people may have concerns and fears about the idea. Talking to people at an early stage is the best way to deal with these concerns. Good communication and imaginative woodland design can usually get round most potential problems.

You need to make a judgement about how much consultation is required. This depends on the nature of the site and the partners involved in the project. If your site is remote and has no significant impact on the landscape then you may reasonably choose to do little more than talk to the neighbouring landowners. However, if housing surrounds your site, or if you have a wide range of partners or sponsors, more formal consultation may be required. This can involve site meetings to discuss the plans or communication with neighbours through phone calls or questionnaires.

SHADING AND TREE SAFETY

Even though it is not a problem likely to occur for many years, your neighbours may well be concerned about trees shading their garden or undermining foundations. When designing a wood, take into account your neighbours and avoid planting large trees near garden boundaries. If your new wood lies on the south side of a property, then consider planting a broad belt of shrubs, grading into taller trees to avoid blocking the sunlight. A similar approach should be adopted if your site boundary is close to a house or outbuilding. Think how large the trees will be when mature and remember that you or your descendants will have to pay the future tree surgery bill to remove overhanging branches.

PUBLIC ACCESS AND SECURITY

If the wood will be open for access by the public, then neighbours may well be concerned about intrusion and the security of their boundaries. If this is the case, then steering the paths away from these boundaries can help avoid this problem. Planting a belt of thorny shrubs at a one metre spacing along a boundary is an excellent deterrent to unwanted visitors, as well as being good for wildlife. Blackthorn, Hawthorn, Holly and Gorse will all do a fine job.

INVOLVING PEOPLE

One of the best ways to involve people in creating a new woodland is to have a tree planting day. Even very small children are capable of planting trees well, given clear instructions and a bit of supervision. It's a great opportunity to get muddy and to hunt for worms in the soil. Planting trees takes up as much energy as attending an aerobics lesson, so plan for an event lasting two or three hours at the most.

Involving children is also an important way of encouraging them to value the new wood and to take care of it. You will probably find that the children know just as much about why trees are important as you do, since schools are very strong on environmental education.

Involving people goes well beyond the planting day. In fact it is something that you have to think about at the design stage. The first issue is that of entrances. It sounds simple, but if you put in a stile then you automatically exclude pushchairs and those people who are unsteady on their feet (four out of ten people over seventy are unable to cross a stile). Instead, why not install a wide access kissing gate that will be suitable for wheelchairs as well? Each visitor will then be able to get into the new wood and decide how far they wish to go according to their level of fitness and the state of the ground.

You could also involve people in choosing a name for the wood, perhaps by doing some research into old field names.

Monitoring how the wood develops over time is also a fine way of sustaining interest. Periodic observations of birds, butterflies and plants in the wood should be recorded and compared. Fixed point photography is also a fine method for monitoring long-term change in woodlands.

Organising events and placing pieces of art in woods can provide a way of drawing visitors who might not otherwise experience a woodland. Sculpture works particularly well in woodland, particularly on the urban fringe. It's for you to judge what is suitable for your natural woodland.

Two young tree planters intent on protecting a young tree. When using this type of tree shelter, make sure that the flared end of the tube is on top. This ensures that the wood does not get chafed as the tree grows out of the tube. Press the tube firmly into the ground and stake.

Left and opposite: Woodland sculptures in Wilderness Wood, Hadlow Down, East Sussex.

41

Native Trees and Shrubs

Many experts agree that true native plant species are those which were present in Britain when it separated from mainland Europe about 10,000 years ago. The marvels of modern technology mean that we can now date the origins of many plants, and therefore establish their claim to native status. There are others whose origins are still doubtful, and whose claims are based on conjecture and personal opinion. One has to draw the line somewhere, however, and the Botanical Society of the British Isles have kindly allowed me access to their database of native British plant species. It is this list that forms the basis of the following pages on native trees and shrubs, and of the Forest Floor section (page 101).

A Guide to Native Species

Opposite: This pollarded Sessile Oak is probably the oldest in England – possibly up to 1,000 years.

The following pages illustrate as far as possible all the trees and shrubs native to Britain. In some cases, such as that of the Willow family, not all the species are dealt with individually, as there are so many. There are many sub-species of trees indigenous to local areas which are not included, due to lack of space. It is also difficult to draw the line between shrubs, large perennials and climbers, but most of the typical woodland verge shrubs have been included.

Many people consider trees and shrubs that have been part of our landscape for several hundred years to be native. These include Sycamore, some species of Willow and Poplar, Rhododendrons and many others. These are not native, some are excessively invasive and destructive, and many exist at the expense of our own native species.

A case can be made for including the White Poplar (*Populus alba*), a very early introduction, and the Sweet Chestnut (*Castanaea sativa*). The latter is neither invasive nor destructive, but rather a very useful plant. It was probably brought to Britain by the Romans, and there is a Sweet Chestnut in England which is a thousand or more years old.

Of course, you can plant any species you wish, but it would not then be a native woodland. Moreover, it is only native species that support the full diversity of life indigenous to Britain. For example, the Horse Chestnut (*Aesculus spp*) which many consider an integral part of our landscape, originates from Mediterranean countries, where it supports innumerable species of wildlife; in Britain it supports only a few. On the other hand, the dainty but tough Birches (*Betula spp*) which were present when Britain separated from mainland Europe, are food, shelter and host to hundreds of species.

If you are considering planting a large area, it is a worthwhile trying to find out what once grew wild there. The type of soil should give you a clue, as will coppices or woodlands nearby. If not, some research into local history might provide information. There is a useful website maintained by the Natural History Museum (www.nhm.co.uk/science/projects/fff), which will give you plant species by postcode.

Alternatively, leave a piece of land fallow for a few years and see what happens. You may get the precursory wild flowers and grasses, followed by some tree and shrub seedlings. My guess is, however, that you are more likely to get a lot of garden escapees plus many invasive and pernicious weeds!

Many naturalists would argue that it is essential that native plants are kept to their original habitats. This is fine in an ideal world, but in a country where almost all the land is either farmed or urbanised, this may not be practical, and it would be a pity to confine beautiful wild plants to the few pockets and remnants that remain. However, if at all possible, collect seeds locally, and seek advice from organisations and suppliers (see pages 118–121).

I have given the final heights and rates of growth over ten years, but these are only very approximate. Climate, soil and management can all affect the rate of growth and final stature of different species, and even their appearance.

Guidelines for propagation are also given. Creating a woodland from collected seeds and cuttings is the most economic way, although you should be prepared for erratic results.

I have also roughly indicated which plants provide food and shelter for birds, moths and butterflies. This is only an indication and you should in no way expect a certain moth or bird to be present just because the food plants are abundant. The complex relationship between all types of wildlife (plants, fungi, birds, reptiles, beetles, insects etc.) and their habitat is not yet fully understood. However, you can be certain that if birds and butterflies *are* present, the insect and other worlds will also be flourishing.

Acer Campestre
Field Maple, Common Maple

Height 6–12m (20–40ft)

Height in 10 years 5–6m (16–20ft)

Propagation Either sow seeds outside in early autumn or soak seeds in warm water for a few hours for spring sowing. Softwood cuttings can be taken in early summer. For best results with fresh seed, warm stratify for four weeks and cold stratify for 10–20 weeks.

The Field Maple is part of a large genus consisting of hundreds of species and cultivars including the Sycamore (*Acer pseudoplatanus*). This is not a native although it has grown here for many years, and it is so invasive that it should not be planted. In any case, the gentler Field Maple is infinitely prettier and more interesting. It is an undemanding tree that will grow anywhere and after only a few years will readily seed itself. It can vary considerably in height and will probably grow taller in slightly alkaline soil. In the south of England some have grown to 20m (60ft) or more.

A ten-year-old tree

The spring leaves of Field Maple are often delicately multi-coloured.

Field Maple flowers in March/ April. They are hermaphrodite on erect corymbs, and the females produce masses of winged seeds (left).

Opposite: Field Maple turns brilliant yellows in autumn.

Alnus Glutinosa
Alder

Height 16–30m (52–98ft)

Height in 10 years 1–2m (3–6ft)

Propagation Sow fresh seed in autumn; alternatively soak dried ones in cold water for 48 hours. Softwood cuttings can be taken, but are difficult to strike.

A very versatile tree which can be planted in wet and boggy soils, or along rivers where its massive root system will help retain banks. It will also grow in very poor soil, as it is a nitrogen fixing plant (one that manufactures nitrogen out of air and stores it in the roots). Once well established, even bouts of drought do not appear to worry it as its root system retains moisture.

In recent years, Alders have been attacked by a fungus, *Phytophthora*. The trees that succumb to this disease are mostly those on river banks, so it may be best not to plant them in these locations. An affected tree, if pollarded, will normally send out healthy shoots.

Alders attract Redpolls and Siskins, sometimes in great numbers, especially in winter. The Redpoll is now an endangered bird, no doubt partially due to loss of habitat. Alders are also a food plant for many moths and butterflies.

Male and female flowers appear on the same tree in February/April. The males are shown below. The females (inset left) look like nuts. Note the new seeds alongside last year's cones. Left: A clump of Alders that have developed naturally in a boggy area.

Berberis Vulgaris
Barberry, Pipperidge Bush

Height 2–3m (6–10ft)

Height in 10 years 2m (6ft)

Propagation Sow fresh, macerated seed in early autumn, or cold stratify for 8 weeks for spring sowing. Cuttings should be taken from fairly ripe wood in late summer and put in a moist atmosphere with bottom heat.

This genus consists of some two hundred species of both deciduous and evergreen shrubs. Barberry was once a common native shrub, but is now more often found in gardens. Barberry growing in the wild was probably largely destroyed by farmers, as the shrub caused wheat rust (*Puccinia graminis*). Do not plant too near to arable fields.

The berries were once used for making jelly and pickled garnishes, and in sweetmeats or comfits. They are very acid and some claim that they are not palatable to birds, although I have seen birds happily strip the bushes in mid-winter. It is a hardy, accommodating shrub.

Berberis vulgaris has insignificant flowers in spring, but these turn into lovely bunches of red berries in autumn (above). It can grow into a dense thicket with sharp thorns similar to its garden relatives.

Betula Pendula
Silver Birch

Betula Pubescens
Downy Birch

Height up to 33m (108ft)

Height in 10 years 5–6m (16–20ft)

Propagation Should not be necessary if other trees in vicinity. If not, soak in cold water for 4 hours before sowing. Cuttings best taken in spring from young shoots.

The Silver Birch and its close relative the Downy Birch (*B. pubescens*) are some of the oldest native trees; hardy, fast growing and tolerant of all kinds of soil and weather. They were one of the first trees to appear in Britain after the last ice age about 10,000 years ago. They are often referred to as 'the forester's weed', and weed they certainly are in some areas! They germinate prolifically to the point of suffocating most other species. I have counted over 123 seedlings and saplings growing in one square metre! Hardly surprising when one birch can contain several thousand catkins and each catkin about five and a half million grains of pollen! But they have many redeeming features, not least their graceful habit, lace-like foliage and arrestingly beautiful white trunks. The Downy Birch is very similar to the Silver: slightly smaller, trunk brownish, and, unlike its cousin, will flourish in very wet and more acid soils. Birches generally live about sixty years.

Birches are home to hundreds of beetles and insects and are the food plant to a host of beautiful butterflies and moths. They include the lovely Camberwell Beauty, which is a migrant visitor, the Willow Beauty, the Lobster Moth which gets its name from the strange lobster-like stance of the caterpillar, the silky-haired caterpillar of the Miller, and the red-spotted Grey Dagger.

Birches hybridise freely and it is often difficult to find a genuine specimen. The above is probably a true Silver Birch.

Right: Birch catkins which could produce thousands of seedlings, in spring.

Buxus Sempervirens
Box

Height 3–5m (10–16ft)

Propagation Sow seeds immediately they ripen, or sow in spring in warmth at 24°C (80°F). If they do not germinate in a month or so, remove to cold (just above freezing) for 1 to 3 months and then back into warmth. Take semi-ripe cuttings, which strike easily.

This evergreen shrub is now quite rare in the wild, but frequently encountered in gardens where it is usually used for the rather unnatural art of topiary. Box Hill in the south of England still has a famous site of natural Boxes. It is a dense shrub which all animals avoid and not even rabbits will nibble it. It prefers calcerous soils, but I have them growing quite happily on clay. The timber, although small, is the hardest of all European species and valuable for wood turners, cabinet makers and for the makers of musical instruments. It flowers in April.

Above: An ancient Box. It will, if left to its own devices, grow into a gangly, sprawling tree.

Far left: Male and female flowers which appear on the same tree in clusters in April.

Left: Seeds ripen in late summer. The seeds and all other parts of the Box tree are poisonous.

Above: Male Hornbeam catkins in winter

Right: The trunk of this small tree snapped off in the 1987 hurricane and has temporarily turned itself into a well-shaped shrub. It will continue to grow as if pollarded.

Carpinus Betulus
Hornbeam

Height 16–30m (52–98ft)

Height in 10 years 3m (10ft)

Propagation Seeds should be collected in early autumn and sown immediately (outside). For best results, warm stratify fresh seed for 4 weeks, then cold stratify for 10–13 weeks for spring sowing. If seeds have been dried, warm stratify for 2 or 3 months, and then cold stratify for 3 to 4 months. Cuttings are not easy to strike.

This is a native of southern England, although it grows as far north as Scotland. It is a handsome tree that turns brilliant yellow in autumn and one that has been much neglected in recent years. This is probably because its wood, mainly pollarded and used for charcoal, has little commercial value today. The wood is very hard, almost bone-like (hence the name) and is still used for piano parts. It prefers moist, well-drained clay soils, but once it attains a good height it will not readily withstand strong winds. On the other hand it readily regenerates and seeds itself prolifically.

Squirrels destructively strip the trunks, as they do those of the Hornbeam's look-alike, the Beech (*Fagus sylvatica*). Male and female catkins appear in March. Hawfinches are partial to the bunches of fruits.

Buds are dormant most of the winter and then suddenly burst into brilliant yellow catkins in spring (top of page opposite). Bunches of seeds form very quickly (top right) and will be ready to pick in October (bottom right).

Overleaf: An ancient pollarded Hornbeam growing in Park Wood, Kent, owned by the Woodland Trust.

Cornus Sanguinea
Dogwood

Height 2–4m (6–13ft)

Height in 10 years 2m (6ft)

Propagation Sow fresh, ripe seed outside, or, if purchased, start cold stratification in summer and carry on for 39 weeks. Softwood cuttings should strike. For best results with fresh seed, warm stratify for 8 weeks, then cold stratify for 12 weeks.

A deciduous shrub that suckers easily, with attractive wood and wonderful autumn colours. It will grow anywhere but especially well on poor, calcerous soils. It is not very drought-resistant, and prefers full sun. The shrub can be found in ancient hedgerows, but is also good for planting along woodland verges. It is attractive to many insects.

The Dwarf Cornel (*Cornus suecica*) is also a native and very similar to to *C. sanguinea*. It is, however, a low creeping perennial.

Below left and below right: White flowers that appear in May/June ripen into bunches of black fruits in October.

Richard Mabey says in his Flora Britannica that the leaves, which turn a lovely burgundy in autumn, 'if pulled slowly from each end, split, leaving a number of elastic tissues joining two pieces. Many children know this trick, and use it to make notional musical instruments'. I have tried it, and it works!

Above: Large male catkins with two tiny but bright red female flowers.

Corylus Avellana
Hazel

Height 4–6m (13–20ft)

Height in 10 years 3–4m (10–13ft)

Propagation Sow nuts in shells outside in autumn (be sure to protect boxes and beds from marauding squirrels and other rodents) or cold stratify for 16 weeks. Take suckers for planting rather than cuttings. Layering works well.

Above right: Hazel nuts in early autumn. Note the catkins already forming at the end of the branch.

Below: Hazel produces a wonderful show of catkins in early spring.

A shrub, once much cultivated, that can provide you with delicious nuts from August onwards – that is, if you can get there before the grey squirrels! The numerous uses to which Hazel was once put have now mostly becomes uneconomic. They were used for thatching, poles and sticks (the wood is incredibly pliable) and in Medieval times they formed the frames for daub and wattle walls. In Kent they were grown commercially for their nuts alongside other fruits.

You can either let them grow into small trees, or coppice them every ten to fifteen years. If coppiced, they make attractive, thick spreading bushes. Hazel is the welcome harbinger of spring, the male catkins sometimes appearing as early as December, shortly followed by the red females.

They are the food plant for a large number of moths including the Buff-tip, Iron and Coxcomb Prominent, Kentish Glory (apparently now extinct in Kent but still surviving in Scotland), Large Emerald and Nut-tree Tussock.

Cotoneaster Cambricus, syn. C. Integerrimus
Wild Cotoneaster

Height 60–90cm (2–3ft)

Propagation If you can obtain fresh seeds, some warm stratification may be required prior to cold stratification. Dried seed: cold stratify for 39 weeks, starting in summer. Take cuttings of semi-ripe wood.

If you are planning a very small natural woodland, consider planting this little shrub. It is not as attractive as its cultivated cousins, but it is very rare in the wild. In 1983 there were apparently only six plants remaining in a site near Llandudno, Wales, but the numbers have now increased due to conservation efforts. It is one of the specially protected plants under the Wildlife and Countryside Act, 1981.

C. cambricus is the only native among dozens of imported species, some of which are threatening to take over, even in the wild. It prefers well-drained limestone, and once established is a good drought-resistant plant. It should be planted along the woodland edges and rides where it will get plenty of sun. You will have difficulty obtaining either seeds or cuttings, but plants can be obtained from the nursery which houses the National Cotoneaster Collection (see Rumsey Gardens, page 121).

Natitonal Cotoneaster Collection

The berries, which can be numerous, are relished by many birds, especially pheasants and lapwings.

Below: Wild Cotoneaster growing in Wales at Great Orme in Caernarvonshire.

Natitonal Cotoneaster Collection

Crataegus Monogyna
Common Hawthorn

Height 10–14m (33–46ft)

Height in 10 years 3m (10ft)

Propagation As soon as berries are ripe, take off outer flesh and sow. For best results warm stratify for 6 weeks and cold for 14–16 weeks. Cold stratify dried seeds for 39 weeks before sowing. Softwood cuttings may also strike.

The Hawthorn (also known as May plus an array of other common names) was principally grown in hedgerows for many centuries. Oliver Rackham reckons that some 200,000 miles of Hawthorn hedges were planted between 1750 and 1850. But you cannot appreciate the true worth of a Hawthorn in a hedge. If permitted, it grows into a beautiful tree, totally shimmering white in spring and stunning in autumn, with drooping branches laden with brilliant red berries, each of which contains several hard seeds. Seedlings should be planted out into the final positions when very young for, despite their tolerance of all soils and drought, Hawthorns dislike being transplanted.

There are many species of Hawthorn, and most are drought tolerant, but only this and the similar *C. laevigata,* Midland or Woodland Hawthorn (pink flowers), are native. It is a tree steeped in folklore, and has been seen as a protector from evil, the crown of thorns, and a magical tree on May Day.

The Hawthorn is one of the major sources of food for birds in winter when other sources are scarce. It is also the food plant of the Lackey and the large Lappet moths, the pretty spotted Magpie, Mottled Beauty and many others.

Traditionally Hawthorn is a symbol of May Day and is supposed to flower by then, but flowering time is controlled by temperature and weather and varies in different parts of the country.

Cytisus Scoparius
Broom

Height 2-4m (6–13ft)

Height in 10 years 4m (13ft)

Propagation Either sow fresh seed outside in late summer or scarify (soak) seeds in hot water and then sow in good warm soil. Softwood cuttings can strike in as little as 4 to 5 weeks.

The rich, glowing yellow flowers of broom are an asset to any woodland. It loves sun, so is best grown in open glades or along verges. In my own woodland, there was no broom until after the 1987 hurricane, after which the plant suddenly appeared out of nowhere. The seeds must have lain dormant for many years, as do numerous other native species, which spring into life when conditions are right. It grows quickly and flowers in two or three years. In eight or ten years it becomes ungainly, with thick woody stems. In open ground it can become quite invasive, but soon disappears once other trees and shrubs begin to form a canopy. Broom is the food plant for the pretty Silver-studded Blue, the Grass Emerald and the Common Heath moths.

Broom is at its best in full bloom in May. Months later, on a warm summer's day, you can often hear the pea-like pods popping and propelling the seeds far and wide.

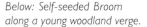

Below: Self-seeded Broom along a young woodland verge.

Above: Seeds emerging from the ripe berries.

Euonymus Europaeus
Spindle Tree

Height 3–10m (10–33ft)

Height in 10 years 2–3m (6–10ft)

Propagation Collect and sow seed outside in autumn. For best results, warm stratify for 10 weeks and cold for 12 weeks. Cold stratify dry seeds for 10–20 weeks for spring sowing. Softwood cuttings can be taken from July to November and strike fairly easily.

Opposite: A mature Spindle tree in autumn.

The wood of this tree/shrub was once used for making spindles, hence the name. It is one of the loveliest of our woodland shrubs. The spring flowers are small and unspectacular, but the leaves and fruit become a stunning, glorious red in autumn. In time the red fruits split, revealing bright yellow seeds. Watch out for this as otherwise the birds will get in first and you will have missed an intriguing sight.

Below: The autumn berries and leaves of the Spindle Tree can be spectacular and magnificent.

The Spindle Tree likes a lot of moisture but well-drained soil.

Above: Spindle flowers, which appear in April/May, are unassuming. The caterpillars of the Carnation Tortix Moth (much disliked by gardeners) sometimes feed on the leaves. Beware: deer and rabbits also relish the young shoots.

Above: Showy male flowers in spring. The small females appear on the same tree.

Below: Ripe Beech nuts ready for collecting and planting. Remove prickly cases.

Fagus Sylvatica
Beech

Height 30–40m (98–130ft)

Height in 10 years 3m (10ft)

Propagation Extract seeds from nuts and sow in autumn whilst fresh and moist; otherwise cold stratify for 12 weeks. Some years masses of seeds are present, in others virtually none. Softwood cuttings are very difficult to strike.

The Beech is an unrivalled tree in spring with its silky grey trunk and brilliant young green leaves – a green which no camera or painter can truly emulate. Few things are more breathtaking than a glade of Beeches just bursting into tiny leaf over a carpet of bluebells (*Hyacynthus non-scripta*) or wild daffodils (*Narcissus pseudonarcissus*) underfoot. Beech is not fussy about soil, but is predominantly a tree from the southern part of England, where it grows on calcerous soil.

In the first years it grows very slowly, but gathers momentum after about seven years. The Beech's great enemy is the grey squirrel, which strips its bark. There seems to be no reason for this behaviour, although some experts believe it is a display of male machismo.

The Barred Hook-tip feeds mainly on Beech leaves. The leaves are also one of the food plants for the beautiful Large Emerald and the intriguing Clouded Magpie, and the fairly scarce Sprawler – a master of disguise.

Opposite: An eight-year-old Beech in spring. It is at this stage, or a few years hence, that the grey squirrel usually attacks the trunk. Retain tree shelters or guards as long as possible, as they seem to deter squirrels.

Overleaf: An ancient Beech, approximately 300–400 years old, in early spring.

Left: The roots of the same ancient Beech.

Frangula Alnus, syn.
Rhamnus Frangula
Alder Buckthorn

Height 6m (20ft)

Height in 10 years 2–3m (6–10ft)

Propagation Sow black seeds (macerated) outside in early autumn, or cold stratify dried ones for 12 weeks for spring sowing. Softwood cuttings taken in June/July may strike.

Despite its name, *Frangula alnus* is not in any way related to the Alder (*Alnus glutinosa*), although the leaves bear some resemblance and both prefer damp, acid soils, and can often be found near ponds or rivers. It is not a showy shrub at any time of year, which may be the reason it is not planted more often. The flowers are minute, and the small berries are snapped up by birds as soon as ripe (remember this if trying to collect seed). The flowers are hermaphrodite.

Buckthorns are one of the food plants of the Brimstone butterfly. Neither the plant nor the butterfly were present in my woods, and to my astonishment, the first year I planted Buckthorn, the Brimstone butterfly appeared. The caterpillars completely denuded most of the small plants, but this, astonishingly, did no harm and the plants are now 3m tall. The Buckthorn is also the food plant of the Green Hairstreak.

Alder Buckthorn flowers are tiny and insignificant, (top right), but the berries in late summer are really pretty, producing many hues in their various stages of ripening (centre right). Bottom right: A nine-year-old Alder Buckthorn.

Long before there are any signs of green, the male flowers (bottom right) appear on Ash trees as tight, red buds in March, to be followed shortly afterwards by the females (above). Ash trees can be dioecious or hermaphrodite. Female flowers (above) quickly turn into bunches of 'keys' (below), and sometimes trees are heavily laden with them whilst neighbouring ones have none. They ripen in September/October.

Fraxinus Excelsior
Common Ash

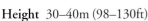

Height 30–40m (98–130ft)

Height in 10 years 4m (13ft) but subsequently grows much faster

Propagation Collect and immediately sow green seed in August/September. If seeds have turned brown, pre-treat with 10 weeks' warm stratification and 10 weeks' cold. Cuttings are very difficult to strike.

The Ash is probably the tallest of all our native trees. Its name, *excelsior* suggests height, dignity and strength, all of which it certainly possesses. The tree is essential to the heart of any woodland. Its light canopy allows sunlight to filter through, which in turn enables many woodland plants to thrive.

The Ash is tolerant of most soils (it grows especially well on lime), but it loves plenty of moisture, and its vast root system feeds avidly. Like most large trees, it grows slowly at first, but after a few years gathers momentum and can grow a metre in one year. Ash leaves are usually the last to emerge in spring, but long before, often unnoticed, male buds form. Both male and female flowers are sometimes on the same tree, the latter producing great bunches of fruits, sometimes called 'keys', which disperse themselves widely and give rise to carpets of seedlings.

The leaves and tender branches are much appreciated by animals. Ash trees are one of the food plants for the Purple Hairstreak, and the Privet Hawk Moth, and once fed the large, beautiful Clifden Nonpareil, now thought to be extinct.

Opposite: Ash trees have a light canopy which permits light to filter through to many woodland plants. The four immense Ash limbs in this picture all emanate from one trunk, 3m (10ft) in circumference. The darker leaves are those of Alnus glutinosa (Alder).

Ilex Aquifolium
Holly

Height 10–12m (33–40 ft)

Height in 10 years 3–4m (10–13ft)

Propagation Seeds are extremely difficult to germinate, although Holly self-generates quite prolifically in the wild. Green cuttings should strike easily and it is also possible to layer in late summer. A long pre-treatment for fresh seed is suggested: 30–40 weeks warm stratification followed by 24 weeks cold stratification.

This tree, deeply steeped in tradition and folklore by Druids, Romans and Christians, is one of our toughest and most tolerant of any soil or weather conditions. It can be a lovely sight in mid-winter when many trees look grey and bereft.

The leaves are thick and glossy with tough spines. Some say the spines evolved to keep off browsing animals, which is why prickles seldom develop on the upper leaves. Others maintain the lack of spines is caused by drought or excessive shade.

Holly is usually dioecious (males and females on separate trees), but some can be bisexual. If possible, only layer or take more cuttings from a female tree, as otherwise you will get few berries. One male tree is sufficient for a dozen or more females. If buying saplings, try to obtain pot grown ones, as Hollies do not like being transplanted. They form a dense shelter for both birds and animals, and a windbreak for other plants, but they also exclude light, so consider carefully where to plant them as little, if anything, will grow beneath them.

Birds love the berries, as does the caterpillar of the Holly Blue butterfly.

Above: A Holly tree survivor of the 1987 hurricane growing among new Oaks and Birches.

Below: Sedate female flowers which will come into their own in winter. Note that the berries are already forming. Inset: A bunch of male flowers. A tree covered with these in spring can be quite spectacular.

Juniperus Communis
Juniper

Height 3–10 m (10–33ft)

Height in 10 years 1m (3ft)

Propagation Only for the super-patient! Seeds take 3 years to mature (only pick black berries), and often another 3 to 4 years to germinate! Cuttings of semi-ripe wood strike fairly easily. Abrasive scarification can speed up germination.

It is a pity that gardeners do not plant more hedges consisting of Juniper, Holly, Beech and other native trees and shrubs, instead of the interminably dull Lawson's Cypress (*Cupressus lawsonia*). Native hedges may take longer to grow, but the end result is well worth waiting for, and they do immeasurable good to the ecology of the environment.

Junipers are not ideal woodland trees, but they will tolerate any kind of soil, deluges, extreme frost and hurricane winds and still come out smiling. They are also extremely useful as windbreaks for less robust plants and shelter for birds in the depths of winter.

Above: Green, blue and ripe black berries on the same tree.

They are normally dioecious and the female trees simultaneously bear green, blue and black berries. They vary considerably in height, depending on conditions, and are one of Britain's only three native conifers.

Unfortunately, rabbits voraciously attack Junipers – as they do all young conifers – and deer are also capable of razing, so make sure you give them protection with a wide tree shelter for several years.

Left: A wild native Juniper stand. There is also a smaller native Juniper, Juniperus nana.

Photograph: Oxford Scientific Films

Above: In October/November black berries form that, in some years, can be quite scarce. The leaves of the true native are narrower than those of the imported variety.

Ligustrum Vulgare
Privet

Height 2–3m (6–10ft)

Height in 10 years 1–2m (3–6ft)

Propagation Soak macerated seeds and sow immediately. Cold stratify dried seeds for 4–9 weeks. Semi-ripe cuttings should strike readily.

The flowers appear in mid-summer and can make quite a show. They produce black fruits that are readily eaten by birds. More important, however, is that it is the main food plant of *Sphinx ligustris*, the Privet Hawk Moth. Hawk Moths are our largest and have beautifully marked soft, furry bodies. The larva of the Privet Hawk Moth is a wonderful spring Beech tree green with lilac stripes, and has the tell-tale abdominal horn of most hawk moths.

Poor Privet! It is the Cinderella of shrubs: it has been ousted from hedges, herbalists can find no uses for it (even Mrs. M. Grieve in her famous, comprehensive *Modern Herbal* ignores it), and people generally seem to be intolerant of it. This may be due to the odour of the flowers which some find obnoxious. Nevertheless, it is worth growing! It can grow into a dense shrub, so do not expect woodland or other flowers to thrive beneath it. The true native is totally deciduous and should not be confused with the oval-leaved semi-evergreen introduced from Japan nearly 150 years ago.

Right: Privet flowers appear in July. They are hermaphrodite, that is male and female in the same flower.

Malus Sylvestris
Crab Apple, Wild Crab

Height 8–10m (26–33ft)

Height in 10 years 3–4m (10–13ft)

Propagation Extract brown seed from fruit and sow immediately.

The wild Crab Apple, pretty on the outskirts of any woodland, is the ancestor of most of our hundreds of cultivated eating apples, as well as the many ornamental cultivars. It is still used as the root stock for grafting new varieties. It existed when the British Isles were separated from mainland Europe, so it is one of our oldest natives.

Below: A Crab Apple tree in full bloom can be a wonderful sight. This one's claim to be a true native is suspect – it may be a hybrid.

Above: Blooms from a true native Crab Apple.

The true Wild Crab can sometimes be distinguished from the many hybrids by its sharp thorns. Blossoms can be tinged pink but are usually on hybrid trees.

The fruits are very bitter, but despite this, jelly, jam and wine are made from them. After the fruits fall in autumn and begin to rot, birds will feed on them avidly.

Pinus Sylvestris
Scots Pine

Height 30–40m (98–130ft)

Height in 10 years 2–3m (6–10ft)

Propagation Collect mature, woody cones, extract seed and plant immediately. You may have to subject the cones to heat in an oven or kiln 49ºC (120ºF) for several hours so they open and spill out the seeds. If purchasing seed, cold stratify for approximately 9 weeks. Cuttings are very difficult to strike, but if attempted, should be taken in winter and subjected to bottom heat.

There are about 117 species of Pine, but the Scots Pine is the only native. It is a native of Scotland, although now planted widely throughout England and Wales. As a survivor of the last Ice Age, it rapidly and densely colonised what is now Scotland and Northern Europe, although those in Europe evolved slightly differently. It will grow in almost any soil. All Pines are monoecious (separate male and female flowers but both on the same tree).

By the seventeenth century, many of the southern forests had been despoiled, so the felling of the Scots Pine began. It was used for iron foundries (in the form of charcoal), pit props, railway sleepers, telegraph poles, and, importantly, for shipbuilding, to fight the wars against the French. Now only remnants of the ancient Scottish Pine forests remain. The reddish bark with its dark crown of leaves make it a handsome, striking tree, especially in the right light (see also page 10).

It is the favourite food of the tiny Grey Pine Carpet and Pine Beauty moths. The latter can become a serious pest in plantations but not, it seems, in native woodlands.

Above: A stand of Scots Pine displaying their wonderful red barks. These trees are approximately fifty years old.

Right: Female flowers come after the males and immediately form green cones which will not produce ripe seeds until the following year.

Below: Male flowers

Populus Nigra
Black Poplar

Height 30–40m (98–130ft)

Height in 10 years 10m (30ft) or more

Propagation If you can get fresh, fertile seeds, clean off fluff and plant immediately. They germinate easily in wet soil. Cuttings of soft, semi-ripe and hardwood will strike.

The Black Poplar is not a very sociable tree. It likes lots of water, yet well-drained soil, and does not really mix well in the forest. It would rather grow alone along river banks. However, as a young tree, it provides a useful canopy for the others as it grows at a phenomenal rate, sometimes one metre (3ft) or more in a year. Do not plant them near buildings, as the vast root system and their insatiable lust for water can cause ground shrinkage.

Black Poplars have lost so much of their habitat through agricultural draining, and indiscriminate felling of so-called 'unsafe trees', that they are now considered one of the most endangered native trees. They are also failing to regenerate themselves, which could be due to the fact that they are dioecious, and mature trees are often solitary specimens with no sexual companion nearby. A number of conservation programmes are now in place, so you should be able to obtain true specimens. There are innumerable, often invasive hybrids.

Poplars are the food plant to many butterflies and moths including the Hornet Moth, Poplar Grey and Poplar Hawk Moth and the White Satin (which has a striking caterpillar – black with white and red stripes), and the Large Tortoiseshell which is now rare in England.

Photograph by Eric Herbert

A five-year-old tree

Above: The female catkins later produce copious white fluff which encases the seeds. Below: The big male catkins, which are 5–8cm (2–3in) long, appear in March/April whilst the tree is still leafless.

Photograph by Eric Herbert

Overleaf: Black Poplars are unmistakable from their arched branches and gnarled, fissured trunks.

Populus Tremula
Aspen

Height 15–20m (49–65ft)

Height in 10 years 10m (33ft)

Propagation Sow seeds as for *Populus Nigra.* Root cuttings give good results.

All Poplars can grow at phenomenal rates, and most prefer well-drained but wet soils. This may be the reason why Aspens grow more frequently in the west and north of Britain. It is a lovely tree throughout the year, trembling grey in summer and glorious amber-yellow in autumn. Male flowers are pinkish, the females grey and silky and both appear (on separate trees) as early as February.

The beautiful Puss Moth feeds on Aspen and other Poplars, and so does the Red Underwing, a master of disguise.

Photograph by Eric Herbert

Above: Young Aspens displaying their greatest attributes – rich golden yellow in autumn and trembling, soft silver-grey the rest of the year. Make sure they are not dominated by taller trees, and that they have sufficient sun.

Photograph by Eric Herbert

Left: Male Aspen catkins

75

Prunus Avium
Wild Cherry, Gean, Mazzard

Height 18–25m (59–82ft)

Height in 10 years 3–4m (10–13ft) or more

Propagation Extract seeds as soon as they are ripe (July) and plant outside. For best results warm stratify fresh seeds for 2 weeks followed by 12 weeks' cold stratification. Stored or purchased seed is difficult to germinate and laborious, requiring soaking and both warm and cold stratification. Cuttings can be taken in spring.

This is a vast genus which includes Plum, Apricot, Almond and Peach trees as well as Cherries. The Gean is the parent of all our cultivated Cherries. It is one of the most beautiful natives, and a very rewarding tree to grow if given space and sun. It is not fussy about soils and in the right conditions will grow very quickly.

Birds, of course, love the fruit. The Brimstone Moth (different from the butterfly) larva feeds on the leaves. It is very difficult to find since it looks exactly like a twig.

Above: Eight-year-old Wild Cherry trees. Make sure you plant trees in groups, otherwise they will bear no fruit.

Below and right: There are many hybrid Cherry trees in the wild, but these blossoms are true natives. It was difficult to photograph ripe cherries: they were there one day and gone the next!

Prunus Padus
Bird Cherry, Hawkberry, Hagberry

Height 10–20m (33–65ft)

Height in 10 years 2–3m (6–10ft)

Propagation As for *Prunus avium*. Semi-ripe cuttings can be taken in early autumn.

The black fruit of this native is far too bitter to eat, but can be used to flavour wines and liqueurs. Numerous cultivars have been developed, but the original is just as attractive. Birds do not hesitate to pluck off the black berries (hence its name). It grows more frequently in the north of England on limestone, but it is not particular as to soil. It is somewhat gaunt when young, but matures into a beautiful, fragrant, flowering tree.

The small Ermine Moth can defoliate a whole tree in summer.

Left: The flowers, like bunches of grapes, appear in April/ May.

Below left: I had singled out a good tree to photograph with fruit. When I arrived, the owners told me I was just too late – two days previously the tree had been whirring with birds! All they left me was a few shrivelled berries!

Below: A mature Bird Cherry in Scotland.

Photograph by Eric Herbert

77

Prunus Spinosa
Blackthorn

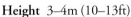

Height 3–4m (10–13ft)

Height in 10 years 2m (6ft)

Propagation Similar to *Prunus Avium*. Cuttings are not really necessary as it suckers prolifically and a small plant can easily be extracted.

The Blackthorn is one of the earliest-flowering native shrubs, and, despite its vicious thorns, it is well worth growing, and not only because you can flavour gin with its fruit. It can be trained as a tree, but is probably best left to its own devices on the edge of a ride or glade. It will grow absolutely anywhere, even on the poorest of soils, and its suckers may have to be kept in check. It forms a dense, impenetrable thicket which is appreciated by birds as a protective nesting site.

It is the food plant of the Figure of Eight, Brown-tail and Yellow-tail moths, and many others.

Above: Blackthorn often flowers in extreme cold, hence the expression 'Blackthorn winter'. The flowers are hermaphrodite.

Below: Traditional sloes for gin and other drinks. There is a Sussex woman's comment about her uncle: 'He likes his women fast and his gin sloe.'

Below, right: detail of the flower.

Pyrus Cordata
Plymouth Pear

Height 3m (10ft) approx.

Pyrus Communis,
P. Pyraster
Wild Pear, Feral Pear

Height 15–20m (49–65ft)

Height in 10 years 5–6m (16–20ft)

Propagation Remove flesh from ripe fruit and plant immediately.

There is considerable confusion about wild pears. Both *P. communis* and *P. pyraster* (extremely difficult to tell apart – the latter has spines) are wild pears but not thought to be native, although they have been in Europe for thousands of years. Oliver Rackham has found references to wild pears dating back to Anglo-Saxon times (see Bibliography). They are not very common, but if planted more widely will make a valuable contribution towards a diverse landscape. Apart from roadsides and hedgerows, they can still be found in some ancient woodlands. They sucker freely.

P. cordata, on the other hand, is considered to be native although it was only discovered in 1865. It is very rare and at the time of writing it is unlikely you could obtain plants, cuttings or seeds. However, several conservation programmes are in hand and the situation could change in a few years.

Above: A young Pyrus cordata *which will never grow into a big tree.*

Left: Fruit of P. communis

Below: P.cordata *in bud*

Flowers of all wild pears appear in April/ May, and the fruits are bitter and unpalatable to humans, but not to wildlife.

Quercus Robur
Pendunculate Oak, English Oak

Quercus Petraea
Sessile Oak

Above: Flowers of Quercus robur *appear with the first leaves in May. The males are large and pendulous, whilst the females are tiny and appear on the tips.*

Height 30–40m (98–130ft)

Height in 10 years 5–6m (16–20ft)

Propagation Plant acorns as soon as they turn brown/black. Soaking for a few hours may help germination. Try to collect seed from good, native specimens. Softwood cuttings taken in summer may also strike.

Keats referred to Oaks as 'those green-robed senators of mighty woods'. Sadly there are few, if any, woods that could be considered mighty, but there are still many powerful individual trees scattered throughout Britain that are some of the largest and oldest in Europe. The literature on Oaks is immense, their properties well known, and no woodland could be called English without them. When planting Oaks, make sure they are true natives, as many current plantations consist of European Oaks. The latter may be better for timber production, but do not possess the squat trunks nor the sturdy (*robur*), compelling limbs of the true English Oak.

There are many hundreds of species of Oak, but only these two are native. They are very similar and at first glance hard to tell apart. *Q. petraea* has leaves and acorns without stalks, whereas the acorns of *Q. robur* are smaller and pendunculate. The English oak grows predominately in the south, and the Sessile is more frequently found in the north.

Neither species is difficult to grow and both support an abundance of wildlife – too numerous to list here. Some say Oaks provide sustenance for 400 species – probably no exaggeration since birds,

butterflies, moths, beetles, insects and mammals all share in the Oak's bounteous gifts. *Flora* also benefit greatly from Oaks, whose leaves rot quickly, providing food for innumerable plants.

Above: A young Oak (Quercus robur) in spring, approximately nine years old.

Opposite: A pollarded Sessile Oak, probably the oldest in the country (up to 1,000 years), named the Queen Elizabeth Oak, as Elizabeth I made a point of viewing this already remarkable tree in Cowdrey Park four centuries ago. It has a girth (still growing) of 13.1 metres (43ft). It now sits, unprotected, in a field grazed by cattle. Note the Butcher's Broom (Ruscus aculeatus), an ancient woodland indicator, growing round the base.

Above: An exaggerated stalk on an acorn, which gives the Pendunculate its name. Sessile Oak acorns have no stalks.

Overleaf: This English Oak is approximately 400 years old. It illustrates all the attributes of a true English Quercus robur: very squat, with a sturdy trunk from which emanate huge limbs.

Rhamus Cathartica
Buckthorn,
Purging Buckthorn

Height 6m (20ft)

Height in 10 years 2–3m (6–10ft)

Propagation Sow collected seed outside in early autumn, or cold stratify dried ones for 12 weeks for spring sowing. Take softwood cuttings in June/July.

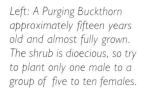

Left: A Purging Buckthorn approximately fifteen years old and almost fully grown. The shrub is dioecious, so try to plant only one male to a group of five to ten females.

Like *Frangula alnus*, this shrub belongs to the family *Rhamnacea*. This seems to be a case, similar to *Betula pendula* and *B. pubescens* where nature in its wisdom evolved one species that prefers to grow on chalky, dry soils (*R. cathartica*), and another that prefers wet, acid soils (*F. alnus*), thus ensuring their widespread survival.

The berries of Purging Buckthorn, as its name suggests, have a violent purgative effect on humans, but seem to have no such effect on birds, who devour them as soon as ripe. The Green Hairstreak, as well as the Brimstone Butterfly's larvae, feed on the leaves of both Buckthorns.

Below left: Like Alder Buckthorn, the flowers of this shrub are tiny and greenish-yellow, but the ripe berries can be very conspicuous.

Below: If the juice is extracted from unripe berries, a yellow dye is obtained, formerly used for staining maps and paper. The bark also produces a yellow dye.

S. Aurita Eared Willow

S. Pentandra Bay Willow

S. Purpurea Purple Willow

S. Triandra Almond Willow

S. Vinimalis Osier

Salix Spp
Willow

This is a very confusing group of trees and shrubs. Not only are there more native species than any other (eighteen in all), but there are dozens more hybrids, as well as countless imported varieties, the commonest being the Weeping Willow. Many Willows were present in the British Isles after the last Ice Age, but as they hybridise so freely, it is now difficult to identify them. All Willows prefer damp, wet soils or to grow beside rivers, streams and ponds. The wood is pliable and accommodating, so for centuries it was used for weaving, and for making furniture and utensils, and, of course, cricket bats! More recently Willows have become popular for weaving living fences, arbours and sculptures.

Male and female flowers should be on separate trees, but there are many exceptions. The outstanding feature of Willows is the ease with which they propagate themselves. They hardly have to contemplate sexual reproduction, as fallen twigs and branches take root so easily at almost any time of year. Anyone contemplating planting willows should acquire cuttings. The optimum time for planting them is winter to early spring.

Eleven species are listed here, but no hybrids. There are also a number of dwarf native species not listed, as they are not very suitable for woodlands.

S. Alba White Willow

Height 33m (108ft). *Ssp caerulea*, cricket-bat Willow.

S. Aurita Eared Willow

Height 2–3m (6–10ft). Prefers acid soil.

S. Caprea Goat Willow

Height 15m (49ft). Leaves more rounded than most willows.

S. Cinerea Grey Willow

Height 15m (49ft)

S. Fragilis Crack Willow

Height 25m (82ft). Twigs snap easily (hence the name). Will tolerate any soil and pollution.

S. Myrsinifolia
Dark-leaved Willow

Height 4m (13ft)

S. Pentandra Bay Willow

Height 18m (59ft). Reddish twigs, glossy leaves.

S. Phylicifolia Tea-leaved Willow

Height 5m (16ft)

S. Purpurea Purple Willow

Height 5m (16ft)

S. Triandra Almond Willow

Height 10m (33ft). The most popular Willow for basket-making.

S. Viminalis Osier

Height 10m (33ft). Widely planted for coppicing and used for weaving.

Overleaf: A lovely example of S. alba (White Willow) which prefers to grow in really wet soils, marshes and streams. It is a large, spreading tree, dramatic in the wind with swaying silver-grey branches. Cricket bats are made from the variation caerulea.

Left: The familiar silky silver 'Pussy Willows' – the male catkins of Salix caprea – make a welcome appearance in early spring when no leaves have yet emerged. They burst into spectacular yellow 'balloons' (above).

Right: Young Salix caprea (Goat Willow), approximately twelve years old.

Below: The less flamboyant green female flowers of Goat Willow quickly turn into fluffy white seeds (below right), which float far and wide. It is debatable whether more trees germinate from these seeds or from fallen twigs striking root.

Sambucus Nigra
Elder

Height up to 9m (30ft)

Height in 10 years 3m (10ft)

Propagation Macerate collected ripe fruit to remove pulp. Allow 10 weeks' warm stratification followed by 12 weeks' cold stratification for best results. Dried seed can be cold stratified for 2 or 3 months followed by a period of warm stratification. Germination in both cases is difficult and erratic. Softwood cuttings taken in summer strike easily.

Richard Mabey describes Elder as a 'mangy, short-lived, opportunist and foul-smelling shrub', which is a little unfair! Elder can look pretty on woodland verges and glades; the flowers provide deliciously aromatic drinks, as do the black berries; and it has myriad medicinal uses.

Elder will grow and colonise anywhere, but especially likes nitrogen-rich soils. They often seed themselves in thick woodlands, where they will never bear fruit – are they perhaps opportunists waiting for a good storm to blow down surrounding trees? It normally grows as a bush, but in sufficient space will grow into a small tree with incredibly hard wood.

Birds eat the flesh of the berries, but drop the seeds, which self-germinate without problem. Many insects benefit from the flowers. The leaves are poisonous, so there is no danger from pests such as rabbits.

Above right: Once the berries are really black, they can be used in cooking and for making wines and drinks. Beware of the green berries (above, centre). They are poisonous and will give you a really bad stomach upset.

Right: Elder blooms in May and the flowers can be the source of excellent drinks (including a type of champagne), all rich in vitamin C.

Sorbus Aria
Whitebeam

Height 25m (82ft)

Height in 10 years 3–4m (10–13ft)

Propagation Similar to *S. aucuparia*. Germination is erratic.

Above: Multi-coloured berries appear in autumn and are much appreciated by birds. Below: Whitebeams grow quickly and should be given as much space as possible. Those pictured are only eight years old, and already add an arresting grey-green hue among the surrounding Oaks, Ashes, Hawthorns and Hazels.

All Sorbus have wonderful berries and year-round interest, but the Whitebeam differs from the others with its furry, white, silky buds and leaves that rival any swaying Aspens or Willows. It will thrive almost anywhere and is well worth planting, especially since Britain's eleven most endangered trees are all varieties of Whitebeam. It is an unusual tree in that it has evolved many sub-species endemic to various parts of the country. They look the same but, to the expert eye, have subtle differences. They include *S. Lancastriensis* (Lancashire and Westmorland), *S. Arranensis* (Arran Islands), *S. Leyana* (Brecon) and *S. Bristoliensis* (Gloucestershire).

Above: Clusters of white spring flowers.

Sorbus Aucuparia
Rowan, Mountain Ash

Height 15m (49ft)

Height in 10 years 3–4m (10–13ft)

Propagation Ripe seed should be planted immediately after removing fleshy outer casing; otherwise cold stratify for three months. Softwood cuttings can be taken in spring.

The Rowan has been associated with witchcraft and magical powers for centuries, and many claim, even today, that it is bad luck to cut it down. Whatever its properties, it is a magical-looking tree with drooping clusters of white flowers in spring and brilliant berries and leaves in autumn. Although it prefers slightly acid soils, it will grow anywhere, even clinging to rocks and crevices high on hillsides, from which it derives its other name, Mountain Ash. It prefers open, sunny positions (lack of sun will affect the colours), and is very wind tolerant.

The berries ripen considerably earlier than the other *Sorbus* species and provide a feast for many birds, including thrushes and redwings. Indeed, birds so love the berries that they were once used as bait for trapping them. Humans too, use the berries to flavour sharp jams and jellies.

Top right: Clusters of white flowers appear in May.

Centre left: An eight-year-old tree, already in full bloom and capable of self-generation. Note that the tree shelter is still present. Rodents readily gnaw the bark at the base of immature trees.

Centre right and bottom: The colour of the berries and autumn leaves can vary considerably depending on weather and soil conditions.

Photograph by Eric Herbert

Sorbus Domestica
Wild Service Tree, True Service Tree

Height 15m (49ft)

Height in 10 years 3–4m (10–13ft)

Propagation Extract the seeds from the fruit as soon as ripe and plant immediately.

The leaves and flowers of *S. domestica* are similar to those of *S. aucuparia,* but the fruits are very different – brown and pear-shaped. Something of a mystery surrounds the tree. It is very rare and slow-growing. Despite its name, *True* Service Tree, its pedigree as a native is suspect. A specimen reputedly three centuries old was found in Wyre Forest, Gloucestershire but, sadly, was destroyed in the 19th century. Luckily, the then Earl of Mountmorris had previously propagated it, so the tree survives today. Later a few stunted specimens were found in South Glamorgan, Wales. These were verified as being truly ancient and related to the one in Wyre Forest.

If you can obtain plants or seeds, it is worth growing if only to ensure its survival outside collections and arboretums.

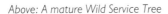

Above: A mature Wild Service Tree

Left: A tree only six years old

Below: S. domestica *flowers in May and produces tiny brown 'apples' in late summer.*

Sorbus Torminalis
Wild Service Tree, Chequer Tree

Height 25m (82ft)

Height in 10 years 3–4m (10–13ft)

Propagation See *Sorbus aucuparia*.

Unlike the previous tree, there are no mysteries about this one, which is a true native. For centuries it was widely grown for its fruits, especially in the south of England. Nowadays it is more difficult to find and deserves wider attention.

The leaves are totally different from other *Sorbus* species. They resemble those of the *Acer* family. Never having consciously seen a Wild Service Tree, I fell into the trap of thinking that quite a number of trees planted in my woods after the 1987 hurricane were some species of *Acer*. I was delighted to discover my mistake.

The Wild Service Tree prefers clay soils, and flowers best in an open position. A mature tree is a wonderful sight in spring when covered in masses of bunches of white flowers, and in autumn when the leaves turn every hue of yellow, orange and brown.

Above: A mature tree covered in white in May/June after the leaves have unfurled.

Left: Brown fruits ripen in autumn at the same time as the leaves turn, often into stunning oranges, yellows and browns.

Taxus Baccata
Common Yew

Height 25m (82ft)

Height in 10 years 1–2m (3–6ft)

Propagation Sow cleaned seed immediately, or both warm and cold stratify for several months. Germination may take 3 years. Cuttings taken in late autumn/early winter after frost strike fairly easily.

An ancient Yew, more than any other tree, exudes brooding mystery, and evokes many emotions with its twisted branches and the permanent dusk beneath its canopy. Many ancient specimens can be found up and down the country, especially in churchyards. The tree is steeped in legend and mythology, both pagan and Christian, and many churches were obviously built in locations where one or more Yews already existed. In Scotland there exists a hollow trunk whose girth was 18m (59ft) in 1769!

Yews are not fussy about soil or situation, but only grow very slowly. Once established, they form a thick canopy under which little else will grow. The tree is dioecious, so the pretty red berries only appear on female trees. The berries themselves are not poisonous, although the seeds are, and despite many stories to the contrary, animals browse the branches from time to time, apparently without any ill effects.

Many birds feed on the berries, and the Mistle Thrush has been known to defend Yew crops from other birds. Surprisingly, the Willow Beauty Moth uses the Yew as a food plant.

Above: A mature Yew, probably about 200 years old.

Left: Male flowers appear on separate trees in March/ April. The females are tiny and green.

Left: Although the seeds are poisonous, birds readily eat the red flesh.

Tilia Cordata
Small-leaved Lime

Height   30m (98ft)

Height in 10 years 3–4m (10–13ft)

Propagation Small-leaved Limes only form seed in Britain in very warm summers, but short softwood cuttings can be taken in June/July, and it is easy to layer them, or propagate from suckers.

It is a pity that nowadays *T. x vulgaris* and *T. x europaeus* have been planted everywhere instead of one of the original, beautiful and historic Small- and Large-leaved Limes. Limes and Elms were once the commonest trees in Britain. They flourished in the warm 'Atlantic' period around 6,000 years ago. Various sites and ancient individual trees have been discovered quite recently, and maybe this will help to bring them out of obscurity. In Westonbirt Arboretum in Gloucestershire there is one which has now been proven to be at least 2,000 years old. Some speculate it is even older. The original trunk has gone but sixty clone trees encircle it.

The Small-leaved Lime produces fragrant flowers in June/July, but ripe seed depends on climate, which at present is often too cold. Tremendous buzzing can be heard in flowering Lime trees – bees congregating for their pollen, to make one of the most delicious honeys available.

The Kentish Glory caterpillar, no longer found in Kent but restricted to Scotland, feeds on Limes and Elms, as does the December Moth, Brindle Beauty and, of course, the Lime Hawk Moth.

Photograph by Eric Herbert

Above: A young T. cordata, *approximately ten years old.*

Left: Limes are one of the last trees to flower.

93

Tilia Platyphyllos
Large-leaved Lime

Height 43m (141ft)

Height in 10 years 2–3m (6–10ft)

Propagation Seed is very difficult to germinate, and if sown as soon as ripe, can remain in the ground for several years with no sign of life. This is on account of its tough, impermeable pericarp that can only be removed with a grinder. Cuttings taken from either Lime species will strike, but dislike being transplanted.

The leaves of *T. platyphyllos* are not that much larger than those of the Small-leaved Lime: in fact, I find it easier to identify it from other Limes, at a glance, as it does not sucker as profusely as *T. cordata*. It grows into a tall, stately tree, towering above all others, clothed in beautiful, dark green leaves.

It is even rarer than *T. cordata*. Both Limes grow on chalk or limestone (I have some growing on clay) but were only widespread in the southern parts of Britain.

Unfortunately, both Lime species can suffer from leaf aphids. These produce copious 'honeydew' which bees collect with the pollen, but which does nothing for the honey.

Limes are very palatable to browsing animals, especially deer.

Above: A mature Large-leaved Lime

Left: Large-leaved Lime flowers. All Limes are hermaphrodite.

Ulex Europaeus
Gorse

Height 2–3m (6–10ft)

Height in 10 years 1–2m (3–6ft)

Propagation Similar to its relative *Cytisus scoparius* (see page 33).

This is really a shrub of rough, open spaces, but, like Broom, its blazing, cheerful yellow blooms can add attraction to the edge of rides. Beware, it is a rampant coloniser – not at all endangered – and can be difficult to remove, its vicious spikes penetrating the toughest gloves. The flowers appear from January to June, and sporadically throughout the year. There are two other varieties: *U. galli:* Dwarf Gorse (a native of the Isle of Man), and *U. minor:* Furze or Whin.

It can grow into impenetrable thickets, which is why birds often choose it as nesting sites, the formidable thorns providing added protection. It is a great favourite with bees, probably because the flowers appear so early.

Gorse is a classic European native which should not be exported to other continents, where it can become as invasive and destructive as the Sycamore in Britain.

The yellow pea-like flowers (left) are similar to those of Broom (Cytisus scoparius). The hairy seed pods (above) can also be heard popping and dispersing seeds in autumn. However, the similarity ends there: Gorse is vicious whilst Broom is positively smooth and gentle. Gorse often flowers in mid-winter.

Ulmus Glabra
Wych Elm

Height 30–40m (98–130ft)

Height in 10 years 3m (10ft)

Propagation If you can obtain fresh seed, sow immediately. Take softwood cuttings in late spring. If taking cuttings or suckers, seek advice to make sure Dutch Elm disease is not already present.

From time to time a totally decimating disease attacks trees. Often, generations later, the cause dies out or the plant develops resistance. Such a blight appeared all over the northern hemisphere and attacked the *Ulmus* species and the related *Zelkova* in the 1960s, in the form of Dutch Elm disease. This is caused by the fungus (*Ophiostoma novo-ulmi*) which is carried by the bark beetle (*Scolytus and S. multistriatus*). The North Americans blame the Europeans for exporting the beetle in logs, and vice versa. No matter who was to blame, the effect was disastrous. One can hope that nature will sort things out, so that one day these beautiful trees can again attain maturity.

You can still grow Elm trees, as the beetle will not burrow into the bark until the trunk has developed sufficiently. Trees will survive at least fifteen to twenty years, maybe longer. Some may avoid the disease altogether. The Isle of Man has an abundance of natural Wych Elms which have been totally unaffected by the disease.

On the positive side, many birds, such as woodpeckers and tits, have benefited from dying Elms; also, luckily, no moths or butterflies rely solely on Elms for food.

Above: Wych Elm is normally associated with Scotland and Wales. This specimen grows in the south of England and is one of the oldest remaining. Alas, despite all efforts by the owners, it seems finally to have succumbed to disease.

Left and above: Purple-red flowers appear before the leaves in spring. The seeds, set in the centre of the fruits, are larger than those of the English Elm.

Ulmus Procera
English Elm

Height 30m (98ft)

Height in 10 years 4–6m (13–20ft)

Propagation English Elms now seldom form seed, but you can propagate them either from suckers or cuttings in spring.

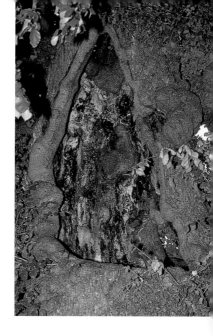

Brighton Council, in Sussex, has been extraordinarily successful in containing Dutch Elm Disease through strict control and monitoring. Although some trees succumb to the disease, many survive, including two U. procera that are up to 400 years old. One is pictured below. Both have mysterious hollow trunks (above).

Most species of Elm are attacked by Dutch Elm disease. The virtual demise of the English Elm in the last few decades has changed much of the countryside. However, Oliver Rackham points out in *The History of the Countryside* that the Elm was always associated with death, and argues that the epidemics of the 1960s and the 1990s could by no means have been the first. Elms once covered about one eighth of the British Isles and were therefore one of the commonest trees, and no amount of Neolithic farming activity could have accounted for the tree's sudden decline. Subsequently the Elms revived, only to decline again centuries later. In Europe, Dutch Elm disease is now in decline. Again, as Rackham points out: 'Elm Disease epidemics have been more frequent and more destructive in the twentieth century: international trade – often unnecessary – disperses virulent strains. The dead Elms of England and New England are both monuments to the unwisdom of carrying coals to Newcastle.'

There are many Elms, but only two others are considered native: *U. minor* (Small-leaved Elm) which grows to about 30m (98ft), and *U. plotti* (Plot's Elm). All Elms prefer moist well-drained soil. The flowers appear in February/March.

Right: A Viburnum lantana approximately ten years old.

Below: The tree bears blooms in April/May which are followed by multi-coloured fruits in autumn (bottom).

Photograph by Julie Wood

Viburnum Lantana
Wayfaring Tree

Height 4–5m (13–16ft)

Height in 10 years 3m (10ft)

Propagation Collect seeds before they turn black and plant immediately, or cold stratify for two months. Softwood cuttings taken in early summer should strike.

Few shrubs rival the conspicuous, shiny berries of *Viburnum lantana* in late summer. They are first green, turn orange/red and finally black. Several colours can often be seen on the same bunch. In spring it bears large heads of uniform white flowers.

The shrub prefers chalk and limestone soils, but I recently planted some in heavy clay where, so far, they are flourishing. The plant is not normally found north of Yorkshire, probably because of heavier frosts, but climatic changes could induce colonies further north.

The berries are very palatable to birds.

Above: Flowers and leaves of the Wayfaring Tree often remain in tight buds for several months in winter.

98

Viburnum Opulus
Guelder Rose

Height 4–5m (13–16ft)

Height in 10 years 2–3m (6–10ft)

Propagation Sow seed when ripe, or both warm (one month) and cold stratification is necessary for dried seeds. Softwood cuttings taken in summer usually root well, as do winter hardwoods.

The Guelder Rose, once called water or swamp Elder, is a lovely native shrub producing masses of white flowers in spring and stunning autumn leaves and berries. Many cultivars are grown in gardens, but to my mind it is difficult to rival the wild shrub.

Once established it suckers freely if given space. It will grow anywhere but prefers moist soil and full sun.

The name Guelder Rose derives from a similar wild tree that grew centuries ago in the Dutch province of Guelderland.

Above: A Guelder Rose only eight years old blooms profusely.

Centre: The showy large outer flowers are sterile, but serve to attract insects, who fertilise the small inner ones, which are fertile.

Left: Leaves and berries combine to put on a dramatic autumn display.

99

The Forest Floor

No woodland is complete without its attendant ground vegetation. Flowers, grasses, mosses, ferns, lichens and fungi are at once charming, fascinating and eerily evocative to anyone who really looks for them. Without them a woodland is incomplete and will not be the habitat for the full diversity of life it should support.

The woodland floor may eventually be colonised by wild species native to the region. In theory, since nearly all the land was once forest or meadows, the flora should reappear of their own accord. In practice, little may grow except coarse grasses and garden escapees, especially if the land was degraded by other uses for generations.

If no meaningful plants colonise a new woodland, and you grow impatient, there is no reason why you should not introduce some, providing it is done sensitively. On *no account* dig up or in any way damage wild species – this would be against the Wildlife and Countryside Act, 1981. Collect wild seeds and try propagating them yourself. There are now a number of nurseries and suppliers who sell both seeds and plants, and some of them will give you advice (see pages 119–121).

A Guide to Forest Floor Plants

Adoxa moschatellina
Moschatel, Town Hall Clock

(P) Height: 4–12cm (2–5in)

This charming plant can grow into large colonies in damp, shady places. It is one of the first spring flowers, coming into bloom in March/April. Four yellow/greenish flowers are arranged at right angles (hence the clock) with the addition of one on top.

The following pages are the merest glimpse of the species that grow in our woodlands, glades and verges. All are native, and have been photographed in my woodlands. In the interests of saving space, the following symbols have been used:

(P) =perennial   (A) =annual   (Bi) =biennial   (B) =bulb

Ajuga reptans
Bugle

(P) Height: 10–30cm (4–12in)

These blue spires will grow both in sun or shade, in grass or light woodland. They are common in damp soils, and have interesting orchid-like 'faces' with white stripes.

Anemone nemorosa
Wood Anemone

(P) *Height: 10–15cm (4–6in)*

Anemones are one of the loveliest sights in early spring woodlands. Huge carpets of nodding heads can cover the ground. They are one of the reliable indicators of ancient woodland. Most are white, but some grow in shades of pink and mauve. They tolerate shade, but will not flower if covered in brambles or similar invasive plants, so these should be kept under control. Alas, they rarely form seed and only expand by rhizomes moving underground at a snail's pace. They are capable of surviving in the ground a very long time and reappear once they can get sufficient light and space. Once the conifers in my wood were blown down in the hurricane, Anemones emerged almost immediately after forty or more years in darkness, and have thrived and expanded ever since.

Angelica sylvestris
Wild Angelica

(P) *Height: up to 200cm (6ft 6in)*

A tall, handsome plant that can be used in cooking like its garden cousin, A. archangelica. It grows in any damp place and is beloved by a host of insects. It is very easy to grow from seed.

Arum italicum
Italian Lords and Ladies
A. maculatum
Lords and Ladies

(P) *Height: up to 50cm (20in)*

These arums are widespread on rich woodland soils. The photographs show A. italicum, and I cannot think why the other is not called 'English' Lords and Ladies, although it does have a host of other names: Cuckoo pint, Jack-in-the-Pulpit, Devils and Angels and more, including a recent somewhat lewd addition 'Willy Lily'! A. maculatum differs mainly in that the spathe is brown and the leaves sometimes speckled purple. The berries of both are poisionous.

Dryopteris spp & Blechnum spicant
Buckler & Hard Fern

(P) *Height: up to 30cm (12in)*

Ferns, beautiful and delicate, are an integral part of any woodland. They can be propagated by spores, or even purchased from garden centres where many are sold as house plants. Make sure they are true native species and not a cultivar or hybrid. There are many varieties, including these two shown in cosy communion. All prefer shade and moisture.

Agrimonia eupatoria
Agrimony

(P) *Height: up to 50cm(20in)*

An intriguing plant that will grow in sun or semi-shade on verges and in grassy glades, especially on calcerous soil. The leaves, not visible in the picture, are pinnate, small ones alternating with a large pair. A. procera is similar and grows on acid soils. The Grizzled Skipper caterpillar feeds and pupates on Agrimony.

Cardamine pratensis
Cuckoo Flower, Lady's Smock

(P) Height: up to 25cm (10in)

This charming plant, said to flower with the arrival of the cuckoo in April/May, grows anywhere damp. It will grow in great swathes in the sun or more sparsely under trees. The flowers vary: white, pink or mauve. Easy to grow from collected seed.

Carex paniculata
Greater Tussock Sedge

(P) Height: up to 150cm (5ft)

A spectacular sedge in maturity, looking as if it had emerged from a tropical rain forest. It grows in very damp, boggy woods of Alder and Downy Birch. The flowers emerge in May/June. The mature 'trunk' becomes like a huge moss pole.

Caltha palustris
Marsh Marigold, Kingcups

(P) Height: up to 40cm (16in) or more

Large clumps of these lovely spring flowers are a wonderful sight. They will grow in sun or shade, but must have plenty of moisture, preferably in a stream or shallow edge of a pond. They are one of our oldest natives and must have grown in abundance before wet meadows were drained for agriculture. I have not seen them in unchecked masses in England, but on similar sites in Canada, they grow almost as far as the eye can see.

Centaurium erythraea
Centaury

(A) Height: 10–40cm (4–16in)

This dainty little flower, together with its creeping cousin, C. pratense, will grow along sunny rides and glades and will tolerate dry conditions. It flowers in mid-summer. The clustered flowers close in mid-afternoon.

105

Circaea lutetiana
Enchanter's Nightshade

(P) *Height: 20–30cm (8–12in)*

If you come across large clumps of this plant at dusk in a woodland, you will appreciate its name, Enchanter's Nightshade. The erect stems stand up like white pyramidal candles in the gloom, and the tiny white blossoms, flecked pink, are enchantment itself. This is not the origin of the name, but for me they conjure up all the mysteries and folklore of woodlands. On the right site, they spread quickly via creeping roots and tend to flourish best on their own.

Epilobium (or Chamerion) angustifolium
Rosebay Willowherb

(P) (A) *Height: up to 120cm (4ft)*

Nowadays many people are disparaging about this plant, doubtless because it is so common and widespread. It is also a great opportunist that, if permitted, will take over any open space (it will disappear in shade). But up to a century or two ago it was considered rare, and a prized garden plant – a classic case of 'familiarity breeds contempt'. The individual blooms are delicate and charming, and en masse, their brilliant wash of colour arresting. Undoubtedly the felling of forest and burning of the cordwood, especially for the two World Wars, had something to do with its population explosion. Few grew in my woodlands until the 1987 hurricane (their cousins were widespread) after which they appeared everywhere. Each plant can produce about 80,000 seeds! Bedstraw and Small Elephant Hawk Moths feed on Willowherbs.

Digitalis purpurea
Foxglove

(Bi) *Height: up to 150cm (5ft)*

This is another plant that will flourish if suddenly given light and space. It will grow along rides and glades, or in semi-shade. Care must be taken when cutting rides, as the following year's plants are already present in autumn. It dislikes chalky soils, and is easy to propagate from seed. The now scarce Heath Fritillary (despite its name it is a woodland butterfly) uses Foxgloves as a foodplant. The butterfly is protected by law in the UK.

Euphorbia amygladoides
Wood Spurge

(P) *Height: 10–20cm (4–8in)*

Euphorbia helioscopa
Sun Spurge

(A) *Height: 10–30cm (4–12in)*

There are a number of Spurges native to Britain, including the pretty Sun Spurge (right) which will grow in the open, and the Wood Spurge which will grow in shade.

Galanthus nivalis
Snowdrop

Ⓑ *Height: 10–25cm (4–10in)*

Although, according to some experts, Snowdrops may not be native, they have been with us a very long time, and their nodding heads, appearing even through snow, are a lovely addition to any wood. They rarely produce seed, but, fortunately, rabbits seldom attack them (they can raze Crocuses to extinction), and bulbs are easily purchased.

Hyacinthoides non-scripta
Bluebell

Ⓑ *Height: 20–40cm (8–16in)*

Bluebells are a spectacular British speciality. They do grow elsewhere, but nowhere in such abundance. En masse in April/May they are an astonishing sight – small wonder that walks and coach trips (even from overseas) are arranged annually to view them. They are tough plants (even resisting rabbits) that grow anywhere in light or shade and will self-seed prolifically providing there is sufficient moisture. Seeds can be collected and germinate easily, but it may take two or three years before they come into bloom.

Lonicera periclymenum
Honeysuckle, Woodbine

(P) Height: climber 10–20m (33–66ft)

The sweet scent of Honeysuckle, especially at night when it attracts many moths seeking nectar, should be present on any woodland verge. It looks wonderful climbing up a tree old enough to look after itself (it will strangle young saplings). It also scrambles along woodland floors where it serves little purpose as it rarely flowers and excludes light from other plants. In sunlight, it will flower all summer and be followed by red berries (poisonous to humans) in September/October. Honeysuckle is also the food plant for many moth and butterfly caterpillars.

Lamiastrum galeabdolon
Yellow Archangel

(P) Height: 20–60cm (8–24in)

As soon as the Bluebells begin to fade at the end of May, the attractive Yellow Archangels appear – like the Bluebells they are an indicator of ancient woodland. They prefer a rich soil, but spread relatively slowly.

Lamium purpureum
Red Dead-nettle

(A) Height: 10–25cm (4–10in)

Red Dead-nettles are common in grass and sunny verges. They are pretty and have a long flowering season, often extending from March till October. Its relative, L.album, White Dead-nettle, appears a little later, but is not native. Dead-nettles are the food plant of the Beautiful Golden and Jersey Tiger moths (the latter is confined to the Channel Islands and South West England).

Lychnis flos-cuculi
Ragged Robin

(P) (A) Height: 30–90cm (12–35in)

I used to find great bunches of Ragged Robin on the verges of my own and other woods, but in recent years they have become progressively rarer and grow more sparsely. Neither chemicals nor loss of habitat can account for this, so I can only put it down to some recent very dry years, and/or wider pollution. It is a cheeky, untidy-looking plant, and you should do everything to further its continued existence. Many moths are attracted to it for its nectar, and it is also a food plant for many caterpillars.

Lythrum salicaria
Purple Loosestrife

(P) Height: 60–120cm (24–47in)

Tall, and stately, Purple Loosestrife is now more often seen in gardens than in the wild on wet ground, and by ponds, rivers and ditches. I grew some from seed one year, but they never flowered and disappeared. I need not have bothered, because I subsequently discovered this clump growing near one of the ponds! Its appearance fluctuates from year to year. The Emperor Moth caterpillar feeds on Loosestrife.

Malva moschata
Musk Mallow

(P) Height: 20–40cm (8–16in)

Musk Mallow usually grows on dry, chalky soil, but those in the photograph were found along a woodland edge in clay on sandstone, successfully struggling through Nettles and Willowherbs. It is an extremely pretty plant, normally with pink flowers (some are also white) appearing in July and August. It is one of the food plants of the Grizzled Skipper caterpillar whose Latin name is Pyrgus malvae.

Melampyrum pratense
Common Cow-wheat

(A) Height: 8–25cm (3–10in)

This species is normally found on sites of ancient woodland. In a good year it will appear as widespread clumps that flower from late spring to early autumn. It is not very common, but other species of Melampyrum are even less so. Cow-wheat is one of the major food plants for the Heath Fritillary.

Mercurialis perennis
Dog's Mercury

(P) Height: 10–40cm (4–16in)

Another plant of ancient woods. It is easy to colonise in a new wood, but beware, it can spread very quickly through underground rhizomes, cutting out light from other plants. It is also poisonous.

Narcissus pseudonarcissus
Wild Daffodil, Lent Lily

Ⓑ Height: 10–40cm (4–16in)

Loss of habitat and the plundering of bulbs must be partially responsible for the decline of this dainty plant, which once grew in abundance throughout the British Isles. Plenty of bulbs are sold under the label 'for naturalizing', or 'Wild Daffodils', but they are not the same. Bulbs of the true native species were at one time difficult to find and expensive, but they are now much more widely available. They will grow almost anywhere, but are especially delightful in woodlands where they flower in March/April before the trees come into full leaf. It takes a number of years before they form goodly clumps, so plant three or four in close proximity. N. obvallaris, Tenby Daffodil, comes exclusively from Wales.

Orchidaceae
Orchids

Ⓟ

I was reluctant to include any orchids since they are very difficult to propagate, and the temptation to dig up these alluring, glamorous plants might just become too great. However, having discovered a nursery that grows genuine wild species (see page 121), I include one of the four I have growing at home. None was widespread until I cleared the Brambles where one or two were growing, and a colony of Early Purples (above – note the uncleared Brambles in the background) have now almost formed a woodland meadow. The Twayblades are also in the vicinity but are less spectacular. No orchids can now be termed common, although these two can still be found fairly easily, but many others are desperately rare, so research their habitats and grow them if at all possible.

Oxalis acetosella
Wood Sorrel

Ⓟ Height: 5–10cm (2–4in)

This is one of my favourite woodland flowers, and I wish it were as rampant as the imported Oxalis species which persistently invade the vegetable garden! Wood Sorrel prefers shady places and rocks, and, in my experience, prefers damp, well-drained soil.

Primula vulgaris
Primrose

Ⓟ Height: 6–15cm (2¼–6in)

Luckily, Primroses are still fairly common. They begin to flower as early as February, and grow best in very open woods or glades with good rich soil. Dry summers and autumns tend to set them back. Other species include P.scotia, native only to Scotland, and the much-loved Cowslip (P.veris,) which flowers best on open, chalky soils. The caterpillar of the grand-sounding, but tiny, Duke of Burgundy Fritillary feeds and pupates on these species.

111

Ranunculus flammula
Lesser Spearwort

(P) *Height: 10–30cm (4–12in)*

Some of the Ranunculus species are very invasive and frequently a nuisance, but this little plant is rarely found except in wet, even boggy areas. Among Sedges, such as here, it will grow upright, but it also creeps along the ground sending out roots.

Scrophularia nodosa
Figwort

(P) *Height: 40–120cm (16–47in)*

I am always astonished to come across these tall, often solitary plants, in the middle of a wood and flowering in late summer when most other plants have decided to seed. 'Fig' is an ancient word for piles, and the plant was once used to help cure that uncomfortable disease. Figwort and Mullein are the main foodplants of the Mullein Moth.

Silene dioica
Red Campion

(P)(A) *Height: 20–100cm (8–40in)*

Spring in woodlands can be better than in any cultivated garden. Snowdrops, Daffodils, Bluebells followed by Red and White Campions (S. alba) as well as Stitchworts, Yellow Archangels, Bugles and others appear in quick succession, producing a spectacular canvas awash with colour. Campions have male and female flowers on separate plants. These and Ragged Robin are the main foodplants of the Netted Pug.

Solidago virgaurea
Golden Rod

(P) *Height: 10–60cm (4–24in)*

The native Golden Rod is not the showy version which inhabits herbaceous borders. The garden variety is an import from Canada (S. canadensis) where it grows wild in meadows and at roadsides. S. virgaura is much smaller and will grow in quite shady, dry woodlands and glades. The caterpillar of the Lime-Speck Pug feeds on Golden Rod.

Tamus communis
Black Bryony

 Climber

It seems that no butterfly, moth or bird benefits from this striking climber, although there are bound to be other invertebrates that do. The berries, only born on female plants, are poisonous and remain well into winter, even in snow. It is attractive scrambling up shrubs and trees on woodland verges. Keep it off very young trees and shrubs, as it can easily strangle them.

Viola spp
Violets, Pansies

(P) *Height: 4–20cm (2–8in)*

There are no less than thirteen species of native Violets, as well as countless hybrids. Although tiny, no woodland should be without their beguiling little faces. Most will flower from March till June and maybe again in autumn, under canopies as well as in verges and glades. If they find a good spot, they spread rapidly. Only one, V. odorata, is fragrant. Viola spp are the main food plants for several Fritillary butterflies.

MOSSES, FUNGI AND LICHENS

As far as I am aware, it is not possible to propagate mosses, fungi and lichens naturally, although they are an integral part of any woodland. However, in time, especially if dead vegetation is allowed to rot, they will appear of their own accord. These pages give you a tiny idea of what you might find.

Key to photographs

1. *Polyporus sulphuraus*
Chicken of the Woods

Fungus

2. *Amanita spp*

Fungus (poisonous)

3. *Eurynchium praelongum*

Moss

4. *Boletus Versicolor*

Fungus

5. *Amanita muscaria*

Fly agaric

Fungus (poisonous)

6. *Thuidium tamariscinium*

Moss

7. *Everina prunastri*

Lichen

8. **Mossy woodland bank**

9. *Lepista nuda*

Wood Blewitt

Fungus

10. *Sacroscypha coccinea*

Fungus

11. *Hericium erinaceum*
Coral mushroom

Fungus (rare)

12. *Lepiota procera*
Parasol mushroom

Fungus

13. *Peziza spp*

Fungus

14. *Polytrichum commune*

Moss

Conclusion

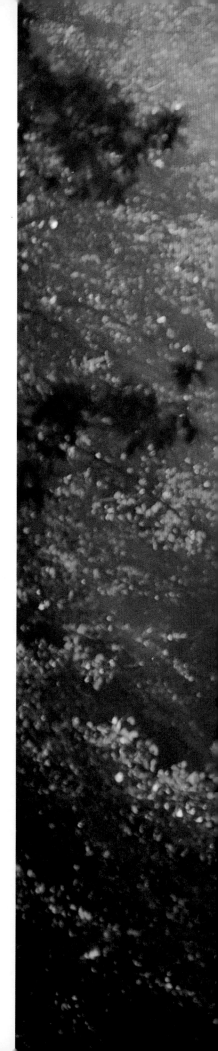

Once a woodland is well-established, it is a matter of philosophy, taste or opinion how much maintenance should take place. Rides and glades will eventually disappear, and with them the attendant flora, unless at least some upkeep is undertaken. In the woodland itself, nature should, as far as possible, take its own course. However, if future generations are going to be able to enjoy fully the beauty of a mixed native woodland, some intervention should take place. 'Foreign invaders', such as Laurel or Sycamore, should definitely be kept out: closely planted trees ought to be thinned; and some species, especially the rarer ones, should be given space and nurtured into full maturity.

Woodland flowers, even our tough ancient Bluebells and Wood Anemones, will not flourish under dense vegetation. They, and others, will bide their time until light re-emerges.

Any trees that die, are brought down in storms, or thinned or coppiced, should be left on the ground to decompose and nourish existing and future plants. If you cannot bear such 'untidiness', at least make piles of the 'rubbish'. It will still rot down, albeit more slowly, but in the meantime it will provide habitats for countless wildlife. On *no account* make bonfires: for many reasons these are dangerous in a woodland, and unnecessarily polluting.

Finally, substantial areas in any but the few-square-metre woodlands, should be literally abandoned to grow into impenetrable thickets. Humans may not be able to enter, but such areas provide invaluable protection for small birds and hibernating creatures, and form additional habitats for inestimable species of wildlife. They will perpetuate and increase the biodiversity which, after all, is the aim of this book.

True natural biodiversity will never be achieved unless linking biological corridors exist throughout the country. I have already mentioned that new native woodlands should, if possible, be planted adjacent to existing ones. Woodlands should not exist in isolation, for many reasons, but most importantly because some flora and fauna cannot traverse farmland, roads and railways. I was recently in Central America, where they have quite advanced plans for establishing biological corridors spanning Panama, Costa Rica, Nicaragua, El Salvador and Guatemala. In the UK a small start has been made by building wildlife tunnels for animals under motorways, but there is no reason why 'plantways' cannot be established above roads, thus linking woodlands and/or meadows. We build tunnels for traffic and buildings, so why not for native species?

The introduction may have sounded pessimistic – a catalogue of what trees, flora and fauna have had to endure. However, nature has incredible powers of recovery: it only needs a little nudge from us humans for it to spring into life and unfold its dramatic miracles. Anyone can extend this helping hand, whether by planting a single tree or an entire forest.

Tree Organisations and Suppliers

This section lists organisations who are willing to advise individuals or groups planning to plant a native woodland. Many of the organisations also have local branches, but only head offices are listed. Organisations marked * may provide grants. Also listed are suppliers of native trees, shrubs and other woodland plants. Many firms will give advice on what to grow in your area, and how. It is advisable to telephone before calling on any of these firms, to make sure that they have what you need.

Arboricultural Association
Ampfield House
Ampfield, Romsey
Hants, SO51 9PA
Tel: 01794 368717
Fax: 01794 368978
e-mail:
treehouse@dial.pipex.com
www.trees.org.uk

BTCV Community Unit*
The Conservation Centre
Balby Road
Doncaster
South Yorkshire
DN4 ORH
Tel: 01302 572200
Fax: 01302 310167
Manager's email:
r.adamson@btcv.org.uk
Adviser's email:
z.suffield@btcv.org.uk

BTCV Conservation Contracts Ltd*
Unit 1a, Treburley Ind. Est.
Treburley, Launceston
Cornwall, PL15 9PU
Tel/fax: 01579 370019
e-mail: contracts@btcv.org.uk
www.btcv.org/contracts

Botanical Society of the British Isles
c/o Dept. of Botany
Natural History Museum
Cromwell Road, London
SW7 5BD
Tel: 0207 9425002
e-mail: ailsaburns@cwcom.net
www.rbge.org.uk/BSBI

Butterfly Conservation
Manor Yard
East Lulworth, nr. Wareham
Dorset, BH20 5QP
Tel: 01929 400209
Fax: 01929 400210
e-mail: info@butterfly-
conservation.org
www.butterfly-conservation.org

Campaign for the Protection of Rural Wales
Tygwyn, 3 High Street,
Welshpool, Powys, SY21 7YD
Tel: 01938 552525
Fax: 01938 552741
e-mail: deb@cprw.org.uk
www.cprw.org.uk

Coed Cymru
Michele Jones
The Old Sawmill
Tregynon
Newtown
Powys, SY16 3PL
Tel: 01686 650777
Fax: 01686 650696
e-mail:
coedcymru@mid-wales.net

Conservation Volunteers Northern Ireland
Beech House
159 Ravenhill Road
Belfast, BT6 0BP
Tel: 02890 645169
Advice line: 0845 6030472
(local rates)
Fax: 02890 644409
e-mail: cvni@btcv.org.uk
www.cvni.org

Countryside Agency, The
John Dower House
Crescent Place, Cheltenham
Glos, GL50 3RA
Tel: 01242 521381
Fax: 01242 584270
e-mail:
robgreen@countryside.gov.uk
www.countryside.gov.uk

Countryside Council for Wales, The (Cyngor Cefn Gwlad Cymru)*
Plas Penrhos,
Ffordd Penrhos
Bangor, Gwynedd, LL57 2LQ
Tel: 01248 385500
Fax: 01248 355782
www.ccw.gov.uk

English Nature*
Northminster House
Northminster Road
Peterborough
PE1 1UA
Tel: 01733 455000
Fax: 01733 568834
www.english-nature.org.uk

Environment Agency*
Rio House, Waterside Drive
Aztec West, Almondsbury
Bristol, BS32 4UD
Tel: 01454 624400
Fax: 01454 624409
www.environment-
agency.gov.uk

Environment Council, The*
212 High Holborn
London, WC1V 7BF
Tel: 020 78362626
Fax: 020 72421180
e-mail: info@envcouncil.org.uk
www.the-environment-
council.org.uk

Farming & Wildlife Advisory Group
National Agricultural Centre
Stoneleigh
Kenilworth, CV8 2RX
Tel: 02476 696699
Fax: 02476 696760
e-mail: info@fwag.org.uk
www.fwag.org.uk

Forestry Commission & Forest Enterprise*
(England)

National Office
Great Eastern House
Tenison Road
Cambridge
CB1 2DU
Tel: 01223 314546
Fax: 01223 460699
Website for all branches listed:
www.forestry.gov.uk

(Scotland)

231 Corstorphine Rd
Edinburgh
Scotland, EH12 7AT
Tel: 0131 3340303
Fax: 0131 3344473
e-mail:
enquiries@forestry.gsigov.uk

(Wales)
National Office
Victoria Terrace
Aberystwyth
Ceredigion
SY23 2DQ
Tel: 01970 625866
Fax: 01970 626177

(Forest Research Station)
Alice Holt Lodge
Wrecclesham, Farnham
Surrey, GU10 4LH
Tel: 01420 22255
Fax: 01420 23653
e-mail: ahl@forestry.gov.uk

Friends of the Earth
26-28 Underwood Street
London, N1 7BQ
Tel: 020 74901555
Fax: 020 74900881
e-mail: info@foe.co.uk
www.foe.co.uk

Institute of Chartered Foresters
7A St Colme Street
Edinburgh, EH3 6AA
Tel: 0131 2252705
Fax: 0131 2206128
e-mail:
icf@charteredforesters.org.uk
www.charteredforesters.org.uk

International Tree Foundation*
Sandy Lane, Crawley Down
W.Sussex, RH10 4HS
Tel: 01342 712536
Fax: 01342 718282
e-mail: hq.itf@tree-foundation.org.uk
www.treefoundation.org.uk

John Muir Trust
41 Commercial Street
Leith, Edinburgh, EH6 6JD
Tel: 0131 5540114
Fax: 0131 5552112
e-mail: admin@jmt.org.uk
www.jmt.org.uk

Native Woodland Trust (Ireland)
Stoneybrook, Kilteel
Co. Kildare, Ireland
e-mail:
info@nativewoodtrust.ie
www.nativewoodtrust.ie

People's Trust for Endangered Species
15 Cloisters House
8 Battersea Park Road
London, SW8 4BG
Tel: 020 74984533
Fax: 020 74984459
e-mail: enquiries@ptes.org.uk
www.ptes.org.uk

Plantlife – The Wild-Plant Conservation Charity
21 Elizabeth Street
London, SW1W 9RP
Tel: 020 78080100
Fax: 020 77308377
e-mail:
enquiries@plantlife.org.uk
www.plantlife.org.uk

Royal Forestry Society of England, Wales & Northern Ireland*
102 High Street, Tring
Herts, HP23 4AF
Tel: 01442 822028
Fax: 01442 890395
e-mail: rfshq@rfs.org.uk
www.rfs.org.uk

Royal Scottish Forestry Society
Hagg-on-Esk, Canonbie,
Dumfriesshire DG14 OXE
Tel/fax: 01387 371518
e-mail: rsfs@ednet.co.uk
www.rsfs.org.uk

Royal Society for the Protection of Birds
The Lodge, Sandy
Bedfordshire, SG19 2DL
Tel: 01767 680551
Fax: 01767 692365
www.rspb.org.uk

Scottish Forestry Trust, The
5 Dublin St Lane South
Edinburgh, EH1 3PX
Tel: 0131 4787044
Fax: 0131 5387222
e-mail: sft@ednet.co.uk

Scottish Wildlife Trust*
25 Johnstone Terrace
Edinburgh, EH1 2NH
Tel: 0131 3127765
Fax: 0131 3128705
e-mail: enquiries@swt.org.uk
www.swt.org.uk

Small Woods Association, The*
The Cabins
Malehurst Estate, Minsterley
Shropshire, SY5 OEQ
Tel: 01743 792644
Fax: 01743 792655
e-mail:
enquiries@smallwoods.org.uk
www.smallwoods.org.uk

Tree Council, The
51 Catherine Place
London, SW1E 6DY
Tel: 020 78289928
Fax: 020 78289060
www.treecouncil.org.uk

Tree Helpline, Arboricultural Advisory & Information Service*
Alice Holt Lodge
Wrecclesham, Farnham
Surrey, GU10 4LH
Tel: 01420 22022
Fax: 01420 22000
e-mail:
admin@treeadviceservice.org.uk
www.treeadviceservice.org.uk

Trees for Life (Scotland)
The Park, Findhorn Bay
Forres, IV36 3TZ
Scotland
Tel: 0845 4583505
Fax: 0845 4583506
e-mail:
trees@findhorn.org.uk
www.treesforlife.org.uk

Ulster Wildlife Trust
3, New Lane
Crossgar
Co. Down, BT30 9EP
Tel: 02844 830282
e-mail:
ulsterwt@compulink.co.uk

Wildlife Trusts, The (46 local branches, phone Head Office for details)*
UK Head Office
The Kiln, Waterside
Mather Road, Newark
Notts, NG24 1WT
Tel: 01636 677711
Fax: 01636 670001
e-mail: info@wildlife-trusts.cix.co.uk
www.wildlifetrusts.org

Woodland Trust, The
Autumn Park, Dysart Road
Grantham, Lincs, NG31 6LL
Tel: 01476 581135
Fax: 01476 590808
e-mail: enquiries@woodland-trust.org.uk
www.woodland-trust.org.uk

WWF
Panda House, Weyside Park,
Catteshall Lane, Godalming,
Surrey, GU7 1XR
Tel: 01483 426444
Fax: 01483 426409
www.wwf-uk.org.uk

Suppliers

Alaska Environmental Contracting Ltd
wild flowers & grasses
Stokeford Farm, East Stoke,
Wareham, Dorset, BH20 6AL
Tel: 01929 463301
Fax: 01929 463889
e-mail: will@alaska.ltd.uk
www.alaska.ltd.uk

Alba Trees plc

trees, shrubs & wildflowers

Lower Winton, Gladsmuir, East
Lothian, EH33 2AL
Tel: 01620 825058
Fax: 01620 825316
e-mail: sales@alba-trees.co.uk
www.alba-trees.com

Ashfield Tree Nursery

*organic trees, shrubs &
wildflowers*

Radnor Support Project,
Wellfield House, Temple
Street, Llandrindod Wells,
Powys LD1 5HL
Tel: 01597 824623
Fax: 01597 824623

Ashlands Trees

*cell-grown tree & shrub
grower*

19 Ashlands Drive,
Leeming Bar, Northallerton,
N. Yorks, DL7 9DF
Tel/fax: 01677 424794
email:
sales@ashlands.demon.co.uk

Ashton Wold Wild Flowers

Ashton Wold,
Peterborough, PE8 5LZ
Tel: 01832 273575
Fax: 01832 273645

British Seed Houses Ltd

Bewsey Industrial Estate,
Pitt St., Warrington,
Cheshire, WA5 5LE
Tel: 01925 654411
Fax: 01925 230682
e-mail: seeds@bshwarr.co.uk
www.britishseedhouses.com

British Wild Flower Plants

flowers & grasses

31 Main Road, North
Burlingham, Norwich, Norfolk,
NR13 4TA
Tel: 01603 716615
Fax: 01603 716615
e-mail:
linda@wildflowers.co.uk
www.wildflowers.co.uk

Burntwood Nurseries

*cell-grown trees & shrubs,
many from SSSI & NNR
sites, all origins known*

The Estate Office, Burntwood,
Winchester, Hampshire,
SO21 1AF
Tel: 01962 882384
Fax: 01962 886788
e-mail:
burntwoodnursery@aol.com

Cheviot Trees Ltd

*trees, shrubs, planting
accessories and protection
materials*

Newton Brae, Foulden,
Berwick-upon-Tweed,
TD15 1UL
Tel: 01289 386755
Fax: 01289 386750
e-mail: sales@cheviot-
trees.co.uk
www.cheviot-trees.co.uk

Chiltern Seeds

Bortree Stile, Ulverston,
Cumbria, LA12 7BP
Tel: 01229 581137
Fax: 01229 584549
e-mail:
info@chilternseeds.co.uk
www.chilternseeds.co.uk

Christie-Elite Nurseries

*trees & shrubs, origin
known*

Forres, Moray IV36 3TW
Tel: 01309 672633
Fax: 01309 676846
e-mail: celite@globalnet.co.uk

Country Flowers Wild Flower Nursery

*flowers: seed, wildflower
plugs; mail order available*

62 Lower Sands, Dymchurch,
Romney Marsh, Kent
TN29 0NF
Tel: 01303 873052

Ecoseeds Ltd

*Irish native flowers grown
using organic, peat-free
methods*

1 Bar View Cottages, Shore
Road, Strangford, Co. Down,
Northern Ireland, BT30 7NN
Tel/fax: 02844 881227
e-mail: eco-
seeds@strangford.fsnet.co.uk

Emorsgate Seeds

flowers & grasses

Limes Farm, Tilney All Saints,
King's Lynn, Norfolk PE34 4RT
Tel: 01553 829028
Fax: 01553 829803

Flower Farms

*flowers & grasses, seed &
plugs*

Carvers Hill Farm, Shalbourne,
Marlborough, Wiltshire,
SN8 3PS
Tel: 01672 870782
Fax: 01672 870782
e-mail:
flower.farms@farmersweekly.net

Forestart Ltd

tree & shrub seed

Church Farm, Hadnall,
Shrewsbury, SY4 4AQ
Tel: 01939 210638
Fax: 01939 210563
e-mail: sales@forestart.co.uk
www.forestart.co.uk

Heritage Seeds

Osmington, Weymouth,
Dorset, DT3 6EX
Tel: 01305 834504
Fax: 01305 834075
e-mail: gd.russell@talk21.com

John Chambers Wild Flower Seeds

15 Westleigh Road, Barton
Seagrave, Kettering,
Northamptonshire
NN15 5AJ
Tel: 01933 652562
Fax: 01933 652576

John Shipton

bulbs, flowers & ferns

Y Felin, Hellan Armgoed,
Whitland, Carmarthenshire,
SA34 0DL
Tel: 01994 240125
Fax: 01994 241180
e-mail: bluebell@zoo.co.uk

Kingsdown Nurseries

trees, shrubs & wildflowers

Kingsdown Lane, Blunsdon,
Swindon SN2 4DL
Tel: 01793 705290

Landlife

*wildflowers, seeds & plants;
visitor centre*

National Wildflower Centre,
Court Hey Park, Liverpool
L16 3NA
Tel: 0151 7371819
Fax: 0151 7371820
e-mail: info@landlife.org.uk
www.landlife.org.uk

Maelor Nurseries Limited

trees & shrubs

Fields Farm, Bronington,
Whitchurch, Shropshire SY13
3HZ
Tel: 01948 710606
Fax: 01948 710440
e-mail: sales@maelor.co.uk
www.maelor.co.uk

Merton Hall Pond Ltd
aquatics (wholesalers)

Merton Estate Office, Merton,
Thetford, Norfolk IP25 6QH
Tel: 01953 881763
Fax: 01953 884020
e-mail:
engs@mhp.newnet.co.uk
www.mhp-ltd.co.uk

Mike Handyside Wild Flowers

15 The Old Paddock,
Main Road, Goostrey, Crewe,
Cheshire, CW4 8QZ
Tel: 01477 549336

Mike Mullis – Wildflower Plants
Weald of Sussex and Kent wildflowers and seeds

27 Stream Farm Cottages,
Netherfield Road, Battle, East
Sussex, TN33 0HH
Tel: 01424 773092
e-mail:
mm.wfp@mullis27.fsnet.co.uk

Mike Thorn
wildflower seeds, plants and bulbs

Branas, Llandderfel,
Gwynedd, LL23 7RF
Tel: 01678 530427

Mires Beck Nursery
flowers & grasses, Yorkshire native origin

Low Mill Lane, North Cave,
Brough, East Yorkshire HU15
2NR
Tel: 01430 421543
Fax: 01430 421543

Mount Pleasant Trees
trees and shrubs, especially Black Poplar

Rockhampton, Berkeley,
Gloucestershire, GL13 9DU
Tel: 01454 260348

Murray Maclean
tree and shrub grower

Collins Farm, Frilford,
Abingdon, Oxon OX13 5NX
Tel: 01865 391242
Fax: 01865 391055

Natural Selection
unusual British natives and seed

1 Station Cottages,
Hullavington, Chippenham,
Wiltshire, SN14 6ET
Tel: 01666 837369
e-mail:
martin@worldmutation.demon.co.uk
www.worldmutation.demon.co.uk

Natural Surroundings
trees, shrubs, ferns, wildflowers, bulbs, seeds, meadow grasses; mail order available

Bayfield Estate, Holt, Norfolk,
NR25 7JN
Tel/fax: 01263 711091
e-mail:
loosley@farmersweekly.net
www.hartlana.co.uk/natural

Naturescape
trees, shrubs, seeds, plugs, aquatics; visitor centre

Little Orchard, Whatton, Notts.
NG13 9EP
Tel: 01949 851045
Fax: 01949 850431
e-mail:
sales@naturescape.co.uk
www.naturescape.co.uk

Organic Trees
trees & shrubs

Doire-na-Mairst, Morvern, by
Oban, Argyll PA34 5XE
Tel: 01967 421203
Fax: 01967 421327
e-mail: raRoy.hills@cix.co.uk

Oxford Tree Seeds
trees & shrubs

11 Spring Lane, Watlington,
Oxfordshire OX49 5QL
Tel: 01491 612014
e-mail:
J.M.Brannan@Btinternet.com

Perryfields Holdings Ltd
flowers & grasses

Inkberrow, Worcestershire,
WR7 4LJ
Tel: 01386 793135
Fax: 01385 792715
e-mail:
amenity@perryfields.co.uk
www.perryfields.co.uk

Poyntzfield Herb Nursery
shrubs, wildflowers, grasses & ferns - Scottish & Highland

Black Isle, By Dingwall, Ross-
shire, IV7 8LX
Tel/fax: 01381 610352
e-mail:
info@poyntzfieldherbs.co.uk
www.poyntzfieldherbs.co.uk

Really Wild Flowers/HV Horticulture Ltd
flowers, bulbs, orchids & woodland seed mixes

Spring Mead, Bedchester,
Shaftesbury, Dorset, SP7 0JU
Tel: 01747 811778
Fax: 01747 811499
e-mail: RWFlowers@aol.com
www.reallywildflowers.co.uk

Rumsey Gardens
Cotoneaster cambricus only

117 Drift Road, Clanfield
Hampshire, PO8 OPD
Tel: 02392 593367
email: info@rumsey-
gardens.co.uk
www.rumsey-gardens.co.uk

Ulster Native Trees
67 Temple Rise,
Templepatrick, Ballyclare,
County Antrim, BT39 0AG
Tel: 028 94433068
e-mail:
neville.mckee@amserve.net

Watermeadow Nursery
aquatics grower

Cheriton, Alresford, Hants
Tel: 01962 771895

Weald Meadows Initiative
flowers & grasses - meadow plants for the Weald area

High Weald AONB Unit,
Corner Farm, Hastings Road,
Flimwell, East Sussex, TN5
7PR
Tel: 01580 879500
Fax: 01580 879499
e-mail:
meadows@highweald.org.uk
www.highweald.org.uk

Wyevale Transplants (Forestry) Ltd
trees, Black poplar specialists

Kings Acre, Hereford, HR4
7AY
Tel: 01432 352255
Fax: 01432 274023
e-mail: wyevale@demon.co.uk

Y.S.J. Seeds Kingsfield Conservation Nursery
trees, shrubs, flowers, grasses, ferns

Broadenham Lane, Winsham,
Chard, Somerset, TA20 4JF
Tel/fax: 01460 30070
e-mail: ysjseeds@aol.com

Yellow Flag Wildflowers
trees, shrubs, wildflowers & grasses

8 Plock Court, Longford,
Gloucester, GL2 9DW
Tel: 01452 311525
Fax: 01452 311525

Glossary

Bisexual (*See* **Hermaphrodite**) A flower bearing both male and female reproductive organs.

Coppice *vb.* To cut trees or shrubs just above ground level to promote the growth of several stems.

Corymb A cluster of flowers where the outer stalks are much longer than the inner ones.

Dioecious Male and female flowers are on separate plants.

Hermaphrodite Flowers with male and female organs on the same flower head.

Humus Decomposed vegetative organic material.

Layer To induce roots to grow by pegging a stem into the soil while still attached to the parent plant.

Maceration Removing the fleshy outer casings from the fruits of certain trees and shrubs before sowing. Large quantities are usually done by machine, but small quantities can be done by hand.

Monoecious Male and female flowers appear separately on the same plant.

Pericarp The part of a fruit enclosing the seeds that develops from the wall of the ovary.

Primeval forest An original, ancient forest that has never been cut down. Secondary forest has had a gap in continuity with the original forest, i.e. it has been recreated on bare land that may once have held primary forest.

Pollard *(vb)* To lop trees about 2.5m (8ft) above ground.

Rhizome The thick, horizontal, underground stem of some plants, whose buds develop into new plants.

Rhizomorph The rootlike structure of certain fungi.

Scarification Inducing tough seeds to germinate either by soaking them in water, or by chipping the outer shells or rubbing them with emery paper (abrasive scarification).

Spores Reproductive 'seeds' of flowerless plants such as ferns and mosses, and of fungi.

Stratification Subjecting seeds to cold and/or warmth in order to break down dormancy and induce them to germinate in controlled conditions. This imitates the natural process in which seeds lie dormant in cold, winter soil, and then germinate when the soil warms up in the spring.

Cold stratification: Keeping seeds in a temperature not exceeding 5°C.

Warm stratification: Keeping seeds in boxes of pots at warm, spring-like temperatures. A temperature of 15–18°C is ideal for native trees and shrubs.

Bibliography

Bean, W. H., *Trees and Shrubs Hardy in the British Isles,* four volumes, revised eighth edition published by John Murray Ltd., 1980

Beckett, Kenneth & Gillian, *Planting Native Trees and Shrubs,* Nature Conservancy Council et al, 1975

Blamey, Marjorie & Grey-Wilson, Christopher, *The Illustrated Flora of Britain & Northern Europe,* Hodder & Stoughton, 1989

Boyd, Morton et al, *Forest Nature Conservation Guidelines,* HMSO, 1990

Broad, Ken, *Caring for Small Woods,* Earthscan Publications, 1998

Carter, David, *Butterflies and Moths in Britain and Europe,* Pan Book in association with The British Museum, 1982

Fitter, Richard & Alastair, *British Wildlife,* Harper Collins, 1981

Fowles, John and Horvat, Frank, *The Tree,* Arum Press, 1979

Fuller, Robert J, *Bird Life of Woodland and Forest,* Cambridge University Press, 1995

Garrard, Ian and Streeter, David, *The Wild Flowers of the British Isles,* Midsummer Books, 1983

Giono, Jean, *The Man who Planted Trees,* Peter Owen, 1989

Harris, Esmond, *Trees and Shrubs of Britain,* Reader's Digest, 1981

Hodgetts, N.G., *The Conservation of Lower Plants in Woodlands,* Joint National Conservation Committee, 1996

James, N.D.G., *A Book of Trees,* Royal Forestry Society of England, Wales & Northern Ireland, 1973

Johnson, Owen, *The Sussex Tree Book,* Pomegranate Press, 1998

Mabey, Richard, *Flora Britannica,* Sinclair Stevenson, 1996

McPhillimy, Donald, *The Community Woodland Handbook,* Reforesting Scotland, *1998*

Miles, Archie, Editor, *Silva, The Tree in Britain,* Ebury Press, 1999

Perkins, Benjamin, *Trees,* Century Publishing Co. Ltd., 1984

Peterken, George F., *Natural Woodland,* Cambridge University Press, 1996

Phillips, Roger, *Grasses, Ferns, Mosses & Lichens of Great Britain & Ireland,* Pan Books, 1980

Phillips, Roger, *Trees in Britain, Europe & North America,* Pan Books, 1978

Potter, M.J., *Tree Shelters,* Forestry Commission Handbook 7, HMSO, 1991

Rackham, Oliver, *The History of the Countryside,* J.M. Dent, 1986

Rackham, Oliver, *Trees and Woodland in the British Landscape,* J.M. Dent, revised ed.1990

Rodwell, John and Patterson, Gordon, Forestry Commision Bulletin 112, Creating New Native Woodlands, HMSO, 1994

Robinson, William, *The Wild Garden,* Scolar Press, 1977 (reprint of 1894 edition)

Rose, Francis, *The Wild Flower Key,* Frederick Warne & Penguin Books, London, 1981

Smart, Nicholas and Andrews, John, *Birds & Broadleaves Handbook,* Royal Society for the Protection of Birds, 1985

Stace, Clive, *New Flora of the British Isles* (2nd ed.), Cambridge University Press, 1991

Warren, M.S, and Fuller, R.J., *Woodland Rides and Glades: Their Management for Wildlife,* Joint Nature Conservation Committee, 1993

Wilson, Edward O, *The Diversity of Life,* Harvard University Press and Penguin Books, 1992

Index of Plants

Scientific names are in italics and common names are in roman type. Figures in **bold** denote illustrations.

Acer campestre **22, 26, 47**

Acer pseudoplatanus 13, **47**

Adoxa moschatellina **102**

Aesculus spp **44**

Agrimonia eupatoria **104**

Agrimony **104**

Agropyron repens 28

Ajuga reptans **102**

Alder 18, **48**, 65,105

Alder buckthorn **65**

Almond willow **84**

Alnus glutinosa 18, **48**, 65, *105*

Amanita muscari **114**

Amanita spp **114**

Anemone nemorosa 4, 13, **100–1**, *103*

Angelica **103**

Angelica archangelica **103**

Angelica sylvestris **103**

Armillaria mellea **35**

Arran Islands whitebeam 88

Arum italicum **104**

Arum maculatum **104**

Aspen **75**

Barberry **49**

Bay willow **84**

Beech 1, 4, 18, 27, 37, **62–64**,

Berberis vulgaris **49**

Betula pendula 4, 5, 12, 18, 27, 29, **50**

Betula pubescens 12, 18, 29, **50**, *105*

Betula spp **44**

Birch 44

Bird cherry **77**

Black bryony 29, 35, **113**

Black poplar **73, 74**

Blackthorn **78**

Blechnum spicant **104**

Bluebell 13, 18, 62, **108**

Box **51**

Bracken 13, 28, **29**

Bramble **29**

Brecon whitebeam 88

Briony **35**

Broom **59**, 95

Bryonia dioica **35**

Buckler fern **104**

Buckthorn 19, 34, **83**

Bugle **102**

Bullrush **20**

Burr-reeds **21**

Butcher's broom **80**

Buxus sempervirens **51**

Caltha palustris **105**

Caprinus betulus 18, **23**, **52–54**

Cardamine pratensis **105**

Carex paniculata **105**

Carex spp **19**

Carex spp **21**

Castanaea sativa **44**

Centaurium erythraea **105**

Centaury **105**

Chamerion angustifolium **106**

Chequer Tree **91**

Chicken of the woods **114**

Circaea lutetiana **106**

Cirsium palustre **19**

Cirsium vulgare **19**

Common ash 18, **23**, 26, 31, **32**, **66, 67**

Common cow-wheat **110**

Common hawthorn 22, **58**

Common maple 22

Common yew 18, **92**

Coral mushroom **115**

Cornus sanguinea 24, **55**

Cornus suecica **55**

Corylus avellana **25**, **56**

Cotoneaster cambricus syn.C.integerrimus **57**

Couch grass **28**

Cowslip **111**

Crab apple 19, 36, **71**

Crack willow **84**

Crataegus laevigata **58**

Crataegus monogyma **22, 58**

Cricket-bat willow **84**

Crocus **108**

Cuckoo pint **104, 105**

Cupressus lawsonia **69**

Cytisus scoparium **59**, 95

Dark-leaved willow **84**

Devils and Angels **104**

Digitalis purpurea **107**

Dog's mercury **110**

Dogwood 24, **55**

Douglas Fir 9, 12

Downey birch 12, 18, 29, **50**, *105*

Dryopteris spp **104**

Dutch elm disease **35**

Dwarf cornel **55**

Dwarf gorse **95**

Eared willow **84**

Early purple orchid **111**

Elder **87**

Elms 34

Enchanter's nightshades **106**

English elm 18, **36**, 97

Epilobium angustifolium **106**

Euonymus europaeus 18, 19, **30, 60, 61**

Euphorbia amygdaloides 107

Euphorbia helioscopia   107

Eurynchium praelongum 114

Everina prunastri 115

Fagus sylvatica 1, 4, 18, 27, 37, 53, 62, 64

Feral pear 79

Field maple **22, 26, 47**

Figwort 112

Fly agaric 114

Foxglove 107

Frangula alnus 65

Fraximus excelsior 18, 23, 26, 31, 32, 66, 67

Furze 95

Galanthus nivalis 108, 112

Gean 35, 76

Gloucestershire whitebeam 88

Goat willow **84, 85**

Golden rod 112

Gorse **95**

Greater tussock sedge 105

Grey willow 84

Guelder rose 31, **34**, 35, **99**

Hagberry 77

Hard fern **104**

Hawkberry 77

Hazel **25, 56**

Hedera spp 29, 35

Hericium erinaceum 115

Holly 18, 19, **68**

Honey fungus 35

Honeysuckle 29, 35, **109**

Hornbeam 18, 23, **52–54**

Hose chestnut 44

Hyacinthoides non-scripta 13, 18, 62, **108**

Ilex aquifolium 18, 19, 68

Italian Lords & Ladies 104

Ivy 29,35

Jack-in-the-Pulpit 104

Japanese knotweed 13

Juniper 18, 19, **69**

Juniperus communis 18, 19, **69**

Lady's Smock 105

Lamiastrum galeabdolon 109

Lamium album 109

Lamium purpureum 109

Lancashire whitebeam 88

Large-leaved lime **94**

Laurel 13

Lawson's cypress 69

Lent Lily **111**

Lepiota procera 115

Lepista nuda 115

Lesser spearwort 112

Lichens 18,114

Ligustrum vulgare 18, 22, 70

Lime 93

Lonicera periclymenum 29, 35, 109

Lords & Ladies 104

Lychnis flos-cuculi 109

Lythrum salicaria 110

Malus sylvestris 19, 36, 71

Malva moschata 110

Marsh marigold 105

Marsh thistle **19**

Mazzard *35, 76*

Melampyrum pratense 110

Mercurialis perennis 110

Midland hawthorn 58,

Mosses 18

Mountain ash **33**, 89

Musci spp 18

Musk mallow 110

Narcissus pseudonarcissus 62, 111

Ophiostoma novo-ulmi 35, 96

Orchidaceae 111

Orchids **111**

Osier 84

Oxalis acetosella 111

Pansy 113

Parasol mushroom 115

Pendunculate oak 12, 13, 18, 19, **25, 34, 80–82**

Peziza spp 115

Phytophthora 35

Picea rubus 34

Pinus sylvestris 10, 11, 23, 72

Pipperidge bush 49

Plot's elm 97

Plymouth pear 79

Polygonum cuspidatum 13

Polyporus sulphuraus 114

Polytrichum commune 115

Populus alba 44

Populus nigra **73, 74**

Populus tremula 75

Primrose **111**

Primula scotia 111

Primula veris 111

Primula vulgaris 111

Privet 18, **22, 70,**

Prunus avium 18, 35, 76

Prunus laurocerasus 13,

Prunus padus 77

Prunus spinosa 78

Pseudotsuga menziesii 9, 12

Pteridium aquilinum 13, 28, 29

Puccinia graminis 49

Purging buckthorn 83

Purple loosestrife 110

Purple willow **84**

Pyrus communis 79

Pyrus cordata 79

Pyrus pyraster 79

Quercus petraea 12, 18, 19, *80–82*

Quercus robur 12, 13, 18, 19, **25**, **34**, 80–82

Ragged Robin **109**, 112

Ranunculus flammula 112

Red campion **112**

Red dead-nettle **109**

Red spruce 34

Reedmace 20

Rhamus cathartica 19, 34, **83**

Rhododendron 13

Rhododendron ponticum 13

Rosa spp 2, 29

Rosa avensis 2, 7

Rosa canina 2

Rosa tomentosa 2, **128**

Rosebay willowherb **106**

Rose hips **123**

Rowan **33**, **89**

Rubus fructicosus 29

Ruscus aculeatus 80

Sacroscypha coccinea 115

Salix alba **84**, **86**

Salix alba 'caerulea' 84

Salix aurita 84

Salix caprea 84, **85**

Salix cinerea 84

Salix fragilis 84

Salix myrsinifolia 84

Salix pentandra 84

Salix phylicifolia 84

Salix purpurea 84

Salix triandra 84

Salix viminalis 84

Sambucus nigra 87

Scolytus multistriantus 96

Scots pine **10**, **11**, **23**, 72

Scottish primrose **111**

Scrophularia nodosa 112

Sedges 19, 21

Sessile oak 12, 18, 19, **80–82**

Silene dioica 112

Silver birch 4, **5**, 12, 18, 27, 29, **50**

Small-leaved elm 97

Small-leaved lime 4, 6, **93**, 94

Snowdrop **108**, 112

Solidago canadensis 112

Solidago virgaurea 112

Sorbus aria **88**

Sorbus Arranensis 88

Sorbus aucuparia **33**, **89**

Sorbus Bristoliensis 88

Sorbus domestrica **90**

Sorbus Lancastriensis 88

Sorbus Leyana 88

Sorbus torminalis **91**

Sparganium spp 21

Spear thistle **19**

Spindle tree 18, 19, **30**, **60**, **61**

Sun spurge **107**

Sweet chestnut 44

Sycamore 13, 47

Tamus communis 29, 35, *113*

Taxus baccata 18, **92**

Tea-leaved willow 84

Thuidium tamariscinium 115

Tilia cordata 4, 6, **93**, 94

Tilia platyphyllos 94

Tilia x europaeus 93

Tilia x vulgaris 93

Town Hall Clock **102**

True wild service tree **90**

Twayblade **111**

Typhia spp 20

Ulex europeaus 95

Ulex galli 95

Ulex minor 95

Ulmus glabra 96

Ulmus minor 97

Ulmus plotti 97

Ulmus procera 18, *36*, *97*

Ulmus spp 34

Viburnum lantana 34, *98*

Viburnum opulus 31, *34*, *35*, *99*

Viola 113

Viola spp 113

Wayfaring tree 34, *98*

Wheat rust 49

Whin 95

White dead-nettle 109

White poplar 44

White willow **84**, **86**

Whitebeam **88**

Wild Angelica **103**

Wild cherry 18, 35, **76**

Wild cotoneaster 57

Wild Crab 19, 36, **71**

Wild daffodil 62, **111**

Wild pear **79**

Wild roses 29

Wild service tree **90**, **91**

Willy Lily **104**

Wood anemone 4, 13, **100–101**, *103*

Wood blewitt 115

Wood sorrel **111**

Wood spruge **107**

Woodbine 29, 35, **109**

Wych elm **96**

Yellow archangel **109**

Zelkova spp 96

General Index

ancient woodland 9, 12, 18, 19, 40, 79, 80, 103, 109, 110

biodiversity 11, 12, 14, 15, 17, 18, 19, 20, 28, 116
birds 2, 11, 13, 14, 19, 21, 28, 29, 31, 41, 44, 49, 57, 58, 60, 65, 68, 69, 71, 76, 77, 78, 80, 83, 87, 88, 89, 92, 95, 96, 98, 113, 116
  Hawfinch 53
  Lapwing 57
  Mistle Thrush 92
  Pheasant 57
  Redpoll 48
  Redwing 89
  Siskin 48
  Thrush 89
  Woodpecker 96
butterflies (and moths) 11, 14, 19, 34, 41, 44, 48, 50, 56, 65, 73, 80, 96, 107, 109, 113
  Asian Gypsy Moth 13
  Barred Hook-tip 62
  Beautiful Golden Moth 109
  Bedstraw Moth 106
  Brimstone Butterfly 34, 65, 83
  Brimstone Moth 76
  Brindle Beauty 93
  Brown-tail Moth 78
  Buff-tip 56
  Camberwell Beauty 50
  Carnation Tortix Moth 60
  Clifden Nonpareil 66
  Clouded Magpie 62
  Common Heath Moth 59
  Coxcomb Prominent 56
  December Moth 93
  Duke of Burgundy Fritillary 111
  Emperor Moth 110
  Ermine Moth 77
  Figure of Eight Moth 78
  Fritillary 113
  Grass Emerald Moth 59
  Green Hairstreak 65, 83
  Grey Dagger 50
  Grey Pine Carpet Moth 72
  Grizzled Skipper 104, 110
  Heath Fritillary 107, 110
  Holly Blue Butterfly 68
  Hornet Moth 73
  Iron 56
  Jersey Tiger Moth 109
  Kentish Glory 56, 93
  Lackey 58
  Lappet 58
  Large Emerald 56, 62
  Large Tortoiseshell 73
  Lime Hawk Moth 93
  Lime-Speck Pug 112
  Lobster Moth 50
  Magpie Moth 58
  Miller 50
  Mottled Beauty 58
  Mullein Moth 112
  Netted Pug 112
  Nut-tree tussock 56
  Pine Beauty Moth 72
  Poplar Grey Moth 73
  Poplar Hawk Moth 73
  Privet Hawk Moth 66
  Purple Hairstreak 66
  Puss Moth 75
  Red Underwing 75
  Small Elephant Hawk Moth 106
  Sprawler 62
  Yellow-tail Moth 78
  White Satin 73
  Willow Beauty 92
  Silver-Studded Blue Moth 59
  Willow Beauty 50

canopy 17, 18, 19, 29, 33, 59, 66, 73, 92, 113
community planting 12, 15, 38–41
conservation 11
coppice 20, 29, 84, 116
cuttings 24, 44–99

disease 15, 28, 30, 32, 34–35, 48
  Dutch Elm 34, 35, 96, 97
drought 13, 20, 21, 26, 28, 32, 33, 35, 48, 55, 57, 58, 68

farming 9, 11
ferns 101, 104
fertilizer 20
floods 13
forest floor 11, 13, 15, 19, 101–115
frost 14, 22, 33, 35, 69, 92, 98
fungi 14, 31, 34, 36, 44, 48, 101, 114–115

germination 22, 23, 50, 51, 68, 69, 73, 76, 80, 85, 87, 88, 92, 94, 108
glades 15, 19–20, 21, 40, 59, 78, 87, 102, 104, 105, 107, 111, 112, 113, 116
global warming 9, 33
grass 14, 17, 19, 25, 28, 31, 40, 44, 101

hedgerows 2, 55, 58, 79

herbicide 28

lichen 14, 18, 101, 114–115

maceration 22, 49, 65, 87
management 13, 14, 15, 44
moss 14, 18, 101, 105, 114–115
mulch 27, 28, 29, 32, 33

pests 11, 13, 15, 25, 28, 30–32, 33, 34, 35, 36, 87
  deer 13, 26, 30, 31, 33, 60, 69, 94
  rabbits 13, 30, 32, 60, 69, 87, 108
  squirrels 13, 30, 32, 53, 56, 62
plugs 22, 24
pollution 11, 21
ponds 15, 20–21, 33, 65, 105, 110

rides 15, 19–20, 21, 57, 78, 95, 105, 107, 116
roots 23, 25, 28, 29, 33, 35, 48, 66, 71, 73, 75, 84, 106

sapling 27, 29, 32, 33, 35, 50, 68, 109
scarification 22, 59, 69
seed 15, 19, 22, 23, 24, 44–99, 101, 103, 105, 106, 107, 108, 110, 112
seedling 22, 23, 25, 26, 27, 29, 30, 32, 33, 35, 44, 50, 58, 66
self-sown 30, 33
self-generation 17, 23, 25, 29, 68
soil 18, 20, 21, 22, 23, 28, 44–99, 102, 104, 107, 109, 110, 111
sowing 22, 23, 44–99
stratification 22, 23, 44–99
sucker 78, 79, 93, 94, 96, 97, 99

tree guards 30, 31, 32, 62
tree mats 27
tree shelter 25, 26, 30, 31, 32, 33, 41, 62, 69, 89
tree spat 33

verges 2, 14, 18, 19, 44, 55, 59, 87, 102, 104, 109, 113

wasps 35, 36
weeds 15, 17, 19, 24, 25, 26, 28–29, 33, 44, 50
wildlife 11, 14, 17, 19, 21, 44, 79, 80, 116